I0013146

Ethical AI Design

Balancing Innovation and Responsibility

THOMPSON CARTER

All rights reserved

Table of Content

TABLE OF CONTENTS

INTRODUCTION

The Future of Ethical AI Design"

Artificial intelligence (AI) is no longer a futuristic concept—it is an integral part of our daily lives, shaping industries, economies, and societies around the world. From self-driving cars to personalized medical treatments, from predictive policing to AI-powered tutoring systems, AI is transforming how we live, work, and interact. However, with these advances come profound ethical challenges that demand our attention. As AI systems become more powerful and pervasive, ensuring that they are designed, implemented, and governed ethically has never been more critical.

This book, **"The Future of Ethical AI Design"**, explores the complex and ever-evolving landscape of AI ethics. It delves into the key issues surrounding AI technology, offering a comprehensive and accessible examination of the ethical dilemmas, challenges, and opportunities that arise as we integrate AI into every aspect of our lives. While AI holds the potential to solve some of the world's most pressing problems, its design and application must be guided by principles of fairness, transparency, accountability, and responsibility. This book is a call to action for developers, policymakers, educators, and citizens alike to engage with the ethical implications of AI and take responsibility for shaping its future.

At the heart of this book is the recognition that ethical AI design is not a one-time consideration or a set of rules to follow—it's an ongoing process that requires constant reflection, dialogue, and collaboration across disciplines and sectors. The journey towards ethical AI involves asking difficult questions: How can we ensure that AI systems are fair, transparent, and free from bias? How can we balance innovation with responsibility? What role do developers, organizations, and governments play in ensuring AI benefits all people, not just a select few? What ethical frameworks should guide AI in areas like healthcare, criminal justice, and the environment?

Throughout the chapters, we will explore the evolution of AI ethics, from its earliest conceptualizations to the modern concerns we face today. We will examine the emerging challenges in AI development, including the risks of bias, discrimination, and the need for inclusivity in AI systems. The book will also dive into the ethical implications of **autonomous systems**, **personalized learning**, and **AI in healthcare**, discussing how these systems can be designed to prioritize **human rights**, **privacy**, and **social justice**. The role of diverse AI teams, responsible innovation, and ethical leadership will also be explored, highlighting the importance of creating organizations and cultures that embed ethics into their AI development processes.

The future of AI holds the potential for remarkable innovations, but it is essential that we build AI systems that are not only technically advanced but also ethically sound. As AI continues to advance, the ethical decisions we make today will shape the society of tomorrow. The implications of **AI-driven decisions** are far-reaching—whether in determining who gets access to credit, who is incarcerated, or how healthcare is delivered—making the need for ethical AI more urgent than ever.

This book aims to provide readers with a deep understanding of the **ethical principles** that should guide AI development and use. It is for anyone interested in understanding how AI can be developed and deployed in ways that are **fair**, **inclusive**, and **responsible**. Whether you're an AI developer, a policymaker, an academic, or simply a concerned citizen, this book will provide you with the knowledge, tools, and frameworks to navigate the ethical complexities of AI and ensure that AI systems contribute to a more **just**, **equitable**, and **sustainable** world.

In the following chapters, we will dive into specific areas of ethical AI design, starting with the **fundamentals** of AI ethics and progressing to more **advanced** topics such as **bias detection**, **AI governance**, and **global cooperation**. Each chapter is designed to provide practical insights, real-world examples, and actionable strategies for building AI systems that respect human dignity and promote societal well-being.

AI is shaping the future. As we stand on the precipice of a new era in technology, it is imperative that we approach AI development with care, integrity, and foresight. The future of ethical AI design is not just about creating machines that think—it's about creating machines that think and act in ways that benefit humanity. Through thoughtful, responsible AI design, we have the opportunity to build a future where AI serves as a force for good, empowering individuals, promoting equity, and driving global progress.

CHAPTER 1

Introduction to Ethical AI

What is Ethical AI?

Ethical AI refers to the development and implementation of artificial intelligence systems that adhere to moral principles and respect human rights. It involves ensuring that AI technologies are designed, deployed, and used in ways that benefit society, avoid harm, and promote fairness, transparency, and accountability.

AI has the potential to revolutionize industries and improve lives in countless ways. However, without careful consideration of ethical principles, AI could also result in negative consequences, such as reinforcing biases, violating privacy, or making decisions that harm vulnerable populations. Ethical AI aims to address these concerns and ensure that AI systems operate in alignment with values like fairness, privacy, and transparency.

Importance of Ethical AI in the Modern World:

- **Trust and Adoption**: As AI becomes increasingly integrated into our daily lives, from autonomous vehicles to healthcare and finance, the public's trust in AI systems is paramount. Ethical AI helps build this trust by ensuring that AI decisions are made in a fair and understandable way, reducing the fear of malicious or biased AI applications.

- **Human-Centered Design**: Ethical AI ensures that the systems prioritize human well-being, aiming to assist and empower individuals rather than replace them or harm them. In other words, AI should serve humanity and contribute positively to society.

- **Legal and Regulatory Compliance**: As AI technologies advance, governments and regulators are increasingly looking to set boundaries around AI's development and deployment. Ethical AI design is necessary to ensure that AI systems comply with emerging laws and regulations regarding data privacy, fairness, and accountability.

The Need for Responsible AI: Balancing Innovation with Ethics

Innovation vs. Ethics: The rapid pace of AI innovation often drives developers and organizations to create cutting-edge technologies without fully considering the ethical implications. However, this unchecked innovation can lead to unintended consequences, such as AI systems that discriminate, invade privacy, or operate as "black boxes" without transparency.

For AI to be truly beneficial, we need a **balance between innovation and responsibility**:

- **Encouraging Innovation**: Innovation in AI leads to new capabilities, from personalized medicine to improved environmental sustainability. These advancements should continue, but within ethical boundaries.

- **Ensuring Responsibility**: At the same time, it's crucial that AI systems are developed and deployed responsibly. This means not only considering the technical performance of the system but also the ethical consequences of its use.
- **Ethical Design**: The design and development of AI systems should involve not only data scientists and engineers but also ethicists, policymakers, and representatives from diverse communities to ensure that the resulting systems reflect broad ethical considerations.

Key Aspects of Responsible AI:

- **Transparency**: Clear communication about how AI systems make decisions and what data is being used.
- **Accountability**: Ensuring that organizations and individuals are held responsible for the actions of AI systems.
- **Fairness**: Ensuring that AI systems do not perpetuate or amplify biases and that they are accessible to all segments of society.
- **Privacy**: Protecting individuals' data and ensuring that AI systems respect privacy rights.

Overview of AI's Impact: On Industries, Society, and Individuals

AI has the potential to positively transform industries, society, and individuals in many ways. Here's a brief look at how AI impacts each area:

1. **Industries**:
   o **Automation and Efficiency**: AI is revolutionizing industries like manufacturing, retail, logistics, and agriculture by automating repetitive tasks, streamlining operations, and enhancing decision-making. AI-driven systems optimize supply chains, reduce waste, and predict market trends.
   o **Personalization**: In sectors like e-commerce, entertainment, and healthcare, AI enables hyper-personalization, offering customized recommendations, tailored treatments, and personalized customer service. This enhances user experience and drives business growth.
   o **Innovation**: AI is driving innovation in fields like healthcare (AI in diagnostics and drug discovery), transportation (self-driving cars), and finance (algorithmic trading). These innovations offer the potential to solve long-standing problems and improve the quality of services across industries.
2. **Society**:

- o **Social Equity**: While AI can increase productivity and create new opportunities, it also risks widening social and economic inequalities if its benefits are not distributed equitably. Without ethical AI practices, biases in data and algorithms can lead to unfair outcomes, exacerbating existing disparities.
- o **Job Displacement**: The automation of jobs, particularly those in routine and manual labor, has led to concerns about job loss and economic disruption. While AI can create new job opportunities, it also calls for retraining and reskilling programs to help workers transition to new roles.
- o **AI and Policy**: The role of AI in governance, security, and public life raises important questions about privacy, surveillance, and the potential for manipulation. Governments and organizations need to ensure that AI is used in ways that uphold democratic values and protect citizens' rights.

3. **Individuals**:
   - o **Improved Quality of Life**: AI applications are enhancing everyday life for individuals by improving healthcare outcomes (personalized medicine, early disease detection), offering smart home technologies, and providing virtual assistants (e.g., Alexa, Siri) that help with day-to-day tasks.

- o **Privacy Concerns**: AI technologies often require vast amounts of personal data, raising concerns about privacy and data security. For example, facial recognition systems, social media algorithms, and targeted advertising all rely on personal data, which, if misused, can invade privacy or be used for manipulation.
- o **Bias and Fairness**: AI systems that make decisions about individuals, such as credit scoring, hiring, and law enforcement, must be designed to avoid bias and discrimination. Ensuring fairness in these systems is crucial to ensure equal treatment for all individuals, regardless of their background.

Real-World Example: AI in Healthcare and Its Ethical Implications

AI in Healthcare is one of the most promising and ethically challenging areas. AI-powered systems are already making significant strides in diagnosing diseases, predicting patient outcomes, and personalizing treatment plans. However, the deployment of AI in healthcare brings several ethical concerns:

1. **Improved Diagnostics**: AI systems can analyze medical images (X-rays, MRIs, CT scans) with remarkable accuracy. For example, **DeepMind's AI** can diagnose eye diseases and predict patient deterioration by analyzing retinal scans or other medical data.

2. **Personalized Medicine**: AI is being used to design personalized treatment plans by analyzing genetic data and predicting how individual patients will respond to different treatments. This can lead to more effective and efficient healthcare.

3. **Bias in Healthcare Data**: Healthcare data is often incomplete or biased, which can affect the performance of AI systems. For example, if an AI model is trained on a dataset that lacks diversity in terms of race or gender, it may perform poorly for certain groups. **Racial bias** in medical algorithms has been found to result in underdiagnosis and unequal access to healthcare for minority populations.

4. **Data Privacy**: AI in healthcare relies heavily on patient data, raising concerns about data privacy and consent. Ensuring that personal health data is protected and used responsibly is paramount. **HIPAA** (Health Insurance Portability and Accountability Act) and similar regulations aim to safeguard patient privacy, but the increasing use of AI calls for enhanced data protection measures.

5. **Transparency and Trust**: AI models used in healthcare need to be explainable, especially when they are involved in decision-making that directly impacts patient health. Patients and healthcare providers must be able to trust AI decisions, but black-box algorithms can undermine confidence in AI systems. Ensuring transparency is critical to maintaining trust in these technologies.

6. **Accountability**: If an AI system makes an incorrect diagnosis or treatment recommendation, who is held accountable? This raises questions about the liability of AI systems in healthcare and the role of medical professionals in overseeing AI-driven decisions.

Example in Practice: AI-based diagnostic tools like **Aidoc** and **Zebra Medical Vision** are used to assist doctors in detecting abnormalities in medical images, such as brain hemorrhages and cancers. These tools can detect issues earlier than traditional methods, offering the potential for better outcomes. However, it's important to ensure that these tools are not only accurate but also transparent and unbiased, and that the responsibility for decisions made by AI remains with human professionals.

Summary

In this introductory chapter, we've explored the concept of **Ethical AI**—its definition, importance, and the pressing need for responsible AI design in the modern world. We've seen how AI impacts industries, society, and individuals, and discussed the potential benefits and challenges that arise as AI technologies continue to advance. Finally, we looked at a real-world example of **AI in healthcare**, where the ethical implications of AI systems are particularly critical, including issues of bias, transparency, and accountability.

As we continue through this book, we'll delve deeper into these topics, exploring how to design AI systems that are fair, transparent, and aligned with ethical principles that benefit society at large.

This introduction sets the stage for the broader discussion of ethical AI design throughout the book, balancing the rapid advancement of AI technologies with the need for careful ethical consideration in their development and deployment.

CHAPTER 2

The Fundamentals of Artificial Intelligence

What is AI?

Artificial Intelligence (AI) is the field of computer science focused on creating machines that can perform tasks typically requiring human intelligence. These tasks can range from recognizing speech, understanding language, and interpreting images to making decisions and solving problems. At its core, AI aims to simulate human cognition, enabling machines to learn, reason, and act autonomously.

Basic Principles of AI:

1. **Intelligence**: In AI, intelligence refers to the ability of a machine to perform tasks in a way that mimics human intelligence. This includes learning from experience, reasoning, problem-solving, and adapting to new situations.
2. **Autonomy**: AI systems can operate without human intervention, making decisions based on data and pre-defined algorithms.
3. **Adaptation**: AI can improve over time through experience. Machine learning (ML) allows systems to learn from data, adapt to new information, and enhance their performance autonomously.

Types of AI:

1. **Narrow AI (Weak AI)**:
   o **Definition**: Narrow AI refers to systems designed to perform specific tasks and operate within a limited scope. These systems excel at completing one function but lack the ability to perform tasks outside their defined scope.
   o **Examples**: Virtual assistants (like Siri or Alexa), chatbots, and recommendation systems (such as Netflix or Amazon's product recommendations) are all examples of narrow AI. These systems are highly efficient at their assigned task but cannot perform tasks they weren't specifically trained for.
2. **General AI (Strong AI)**:
   o **Definition**: General AI is an AI that possesses the ability to understand, learn, and apply knowledge across a wide range of tasks, just like a human. A general AI would be able to perform any intellectual task that a human being can do.
   o **Current Status**: We have not yet achieved general AI. It remains a topic of research, and while there are theoretical advancements, general AI is still far from practical realization. However, the idea of creating machines with human-like cognitive abilities continues to inspire innovation in AI.
3. **Superintelligent AI**:
   o **Definition**: Superintelligent AI refers to an AI that surpasses human intelligence in

all aspects, including creativity, decision-making, and emotional intelligence. This level of AI is purely theoretical and has not been developed.

- o **Concerns**: Superintelligent AI presents a variety of ethical, safety, and governance concerns, with the potential to revolutionize (or disrupt) every aspect of human life.

The Role of Machine Learning and Deep Learning in Creating Intelligent Systems

Machine Learning (ML) and **Deep Learning (DL)** are the driving forces behind modern AI applications, enabling machines to learn and adapt without explicit programming. Here's a breakdown of each:

1. **Machine Learning**:
    - o **Definition**: Machine learning is a subset of AI where systems learn from data rather than being explicitly programmed to perform specific tasks. It allows machines to identify patterns, make predictions, and improve their performance over time.
    - o **How it works**: In ML, algorithms are trained on data to find patterns or structures, enabling them to make predictions or decisions based on new, unseen data. For example, a machine learning algorithm could be trained on a dataset of emails to identify spam.

- **Types of Machine Learning**:
  - **Supervised Learning**: The algorithm is trained on labeled data (data with known outcomes). It learns to map inputs to outputs.
  - **Unsupervised Learning**: The algorithm is given data without labels and must find structure or patterns on its own (e.g., clustering, anomaly detection).
  - **Reinforcement Learning**: The system learns by interacting with an environment and receiving feedback in the form of rewards or penalties (e.g., self-driving cars).

2. **Deep Learning**:
   - **Definition**: Deep learning is a specialized subset of machine learning that uses multi-layered neural networks (also known as deep neural networks) to model complex patterns in data. It excels at tasks like image recognition, natural language processing, and speech recognition.
   - **How it works**: Deep learning networks consist of multiple layers (hence "deep") that process data through successive transformations, learning hierarchical representations at each layer. For example, in image recognition, early layers might detect edges, while deeper layers may identify shapes or objects.
   - **Real-World Examples**:

- **Image Classification**: Identifying objects in photos or videos (e.g., classifying animals or objects in images).
- **Speech Recognition**: Converting spoken words into text (e.g., voice assistants like Siri and Google Assistant).
- **Natural Language Processing (NLP)**: Understanding and generating human language (e.g., chatbots, translation tools).

Understanding AI Technologies: Algorithms, Data, and Models

For AI to function effectively, it relies on three core components: **algorithms**, **data**, and **models**. Here's how each plays a crucial role:

1. **Algorithms**:
   - Algorithms are the set of rules or instructions that guide how an AI system processes data. In machine learning, algorithms are responsible for learning from data and improving over time.
   - Examples of popular machine learning algorithms:
     - **Linear Regression**: Used for predicting continuous values.
     - **Decision Trees**: Used for classification and regression tasks.

- **K-Nearest Neighbors (KNN)**: A simple algorithm used for classification tasks.
- **Neural Networks**: Used in deep learning for tasks like image and speech recognition.

2. **Data**:
   - Data is the foundation of AI. Without data, machine learning models have nothing to learn from. The quality, quantity, and variety of data used to train models significantly impact their accuracy and performance.
   - **Types of Data**:
     - **Structured Data**: Organized data (e.g., spreadsheets, databases) with clearly defined fields.
     - **Unstructured Data**: Data that lacks a predefined structure (e.g., text, images, audio).
     - **Semi-structured Data**: Data that doesn't have a rigid structure but contains some organizational elements (e.g., JSON or XML files).

3. **Models**:
   - Models are the outputs of machine learning algorithms after they have been trained on data. A model represents the knowledge learned by the algorithm and is used to make predictions or decisions.
   - For example, a trained **image recognition model** can classify images into categories

(e.g., cat, dog, car) based on patterns it has learned from the data during training.

Real-World Example: How AI Works in Recommendation Systems (e.g., Netflix)

One of the most widely known and widely used applications of AI is in **recommendation systems**, such as those used by Netflix, Amazon, and Spotify. These systems use AI and machine learning algorithms to personalize content and suggest products or media that a user is likely to enjoy based on their preferences.

How it works:

1. **Data Collection**: The recommendation system collects data on users' behavior, such as viewing history, ratings, and preferences. For example, Netflix tracks the movies and shows you watch, how long you watch them, and whether you rate them highly or not.
2. **Model Training**: The system then uses machine learning algorithms to analyze this data and learn patterns. **Collaborative filtering**, one common method, looks for patterns in user preferences. For example, if two users have watched similar movies, the system might recommend content liked by one user to the other.
3. **Personalization**: Based on this analysis, the system can recommend personalized content. For example, Netflix might suggest a new documentary based on your previous viewing habits, or Amazon might recommend products

based on your browsing history and previous purchases.

4. **Continuous Improvement**: The more a user interacts with the system (e.g., by watching content or purchasing items), the better the recommendations become. The system continuously learns and adapts to improve its predictions.

Example in Action:

- When you log into Netflix, the platform's recommendation system might suggest shows or movies you haven't watched yet, but that match your viewing habits. For instance, if you often watch sci-fi thrillers, Netflix might recommend *Stranger Things* or *Black Mirror* based on your preferences.

Challenges and Ethical Considerations:

- **Bias**: Recommendation systems can inadvertently reinforce existing biases, as they are often based on patterns in historical data. For example, if users are overwhelmingly recommending content from specific genres, the system may become skewed towards recommending those genres and overlook diversity in content.
- **Data Privacy**: The recommendation system uses personal data to make suggestions, which raises concerns about how that data is collected, used, and protected.

Summary

In this chapter, we explored the **fundamentals of AI**, including its definition, the basic principles behind AI systems, and the types of AI, such as narrow AI and general AI. We discussed the role of **machine learning** and **deep learning** in creating intelligent systems and how these technologies power AI applications. Finally, we looked at key AI components—**algorithms**, **data**, and **models**—and how they work together to build powerful systems.

A **real-world example** of how AI works in **recommendation systems** highlighted the practical applications of AI in services like Netflix and Amazon, where personalized experiences are powered by machine learning algorithms that continuously learn and adapt based on user behavior.

As we continue to delve deeper into ethical AI design, this chapter has laid the foundation for understanding the technologies that drive intelligent systems and the importance of approaching their design with responsibility and foresight.

CHAPTER 3

Ethical Frameworks in AI

Philosophical Foundations: Utilitarianism, Deontology, Virtue Ethics

To design AI systems that align with ethical principles, it's essential to ground those systems in established philosophical frameworks. These frameworks provide a foundation for addressing the ethical challenges and dilemmas that arise in AI design, ensuring that AI technologies serve humanity in a responsible and fair manner. Here are three key philosophical foundations that guide ethical decision-making:

1. **Utilitarianism**:
   o **Overview**: Utilitarianism, proposed by philosophers like Jeremy Bentham and John Stuart Mill, is an ethical theory that promotes actions that maximize overall happiness or well-being. In the context of AI, this means designing systems that provide the greatest good for the greatest number of people.
   o **Principles**: Utilitarian ethics calls for an evaluation of the consequences of AI systems. Decisions should prioritize outcomes that lead to the highest level of societal benefit, even if they involve trade-offs or harm to a smaller group of people.

- o **AI Application**: A utilitarian approach to AI design might support the development of technologies like AI-driven healthcare systems that save lives or improve treatment outcomes, even if these systems have some potential risks (e.g., incorrect diagnoses or biases). The key is weighing the benefits against the potential harm.

2. **Deontology**:
   - o **Overview**: Deontological ethics, associated with philosopher Immanuel Kant, focuses on the moral duty of actions, regardless of the consequences. It argues that certain actions are inherently right or wrong, and these duties must be followed.
   - o **Principles**: In the context of AI, deontology emphasizes that certain rights and principles must be upheld in the design of AI systems, regardless of the consequences. For example, privacy rights and fairness should never be compromised, even if violating them would lead to a greater societal good.
   - o **AI Application**: For AI systems, a deontological approach would prioritize transparency, accountability, and the protection of human rights. It would require that AI systems always respect these principles, even if it means limiting certain technological advancements or capabilities.

3. **Virtue Ethics**:

- o **Overview**: Virtue ethics, originating with Aristotle, focuses on the development of moral character and virtues rather than rules or consequences. It emphasizes the importance of cultivating traits such as honesty, courage, compassion, and fairness in individuals and institutions.
- o **Principles**: In AI design, virtue ethics calls for the development of AI systems that promote virtuous behavior and align with societal values, emphasizing moral integrity in decision-making processes. AI systems should not only function well but also encourage and promote virtuous outcomes.
- o **AI Application**: Virtue ethics could guide the development of AI technologies that help people make better decisions, foster social cooperation, and encourage moral behavior. For example, AI-driven educational systems could emphasize empathy, fairness, and kindness in their interactions with students.

Each of these ethical frameworks offers a unique perspective on how AI systems should be designed, developed, and deployed. By combining these approaches, AI developers can create systems that are not only technically sound but also ethically responsible and aligned with human values.

Applying Ethics to AI Design: Translating Philosophy into Practice

While philosophical frameworks provide the theoretical foundation for ethical AI, translating these theories into actionable principles for AI design is critical. Below are key ways to apply ethics practically in AI development:

1. **Incorporating Ethical Principles in the Design Phase**:
   o **Value-sensitive Design**: This approach integrates ethical values into the design process from the very beginning, ensuring that moral considerations are addressed as AI systems are being created. Designers, engineers, and stakeholders should engage in discussions about the ethical implications of AI features, capabilities, and potential consequences.
   o **Risk Assessment and Mitigation**: Conducting ethical risk assessments involves identifying potential harms and ensuring that AI systems are designed to avoid or minimize these risks. For example, assessing the risks of biased outcomes in machine learning models and taking steps to mitigate them (e.g., through fairness constraints or diverse data collection).
2. **Ensuring Transparency and Explainability**:
   o **Explainable AI (XAI)**: As AI systems become more complex, it's important to make sure that their decision-making

processes are transparent and understandable to both developers and end-users. This means designing models that can explain how and why a certain decision or recommendation was made.

- o **Ethical Considerations**: Ensuring transparency also involves making AI systems' capabilities and limitations clear to users, preventing misuse, and fostering trust. Users should understand when they are interacting with AI systems and the data these systems rely on.

3. **Prioritizing Fairness and Equity**:
   - o AI systems should be designed to treat all individuals and groups fairly, avoiding discrimination or reinforcing societal biases. Developers must ensure that the training data used to build these models is representative and free of bias, and that the algorithms themselves do not perpetuate existing inequalities.
   - o **Fairness-Driven Development**: Implementing fairness constraints and continuously auditing models for bias can help to ensure that AI systems are equitable. Tools like **AI Fairness 360** (IBM) or **Fairness Indicators** (Google) can be used to assess the fairness of AI models.

4. **Promoting Accountability and Responsibility**:
   - o Clear accountability structures should be established to determine who is responsible when an AI system makes a

harmful decision or causes unintended consequences. Organizations must ensure that AI systems are subject to regular audits and oversight, especially when they impact critical areas like healthcare, justice, or employment.

o **Ethical Decision-Making Frameworks**: Ensuring that AI decision-making processes are subject to ethical review and align with established moral principles is essential. This involves creating governance structures that oversee AI development, deployment, and use.

AI Guidelines and Frameworks: Existing Global Standards and Policies

Several international organizations and governments have developed guidelines, policies, and frameworks to ensure the ethical design and deployment of AI. Here are some key examples:

1. **European Union (EU)**:
   o The EU has developed the **Artificial Intelligence Act**, which outlines regulations for the development, deployment, and use of AI systems within the EU. This act aims to ensure that AI systems are transparent, non-discriminatory, and respect human rights. It includes provisions for risk

assessments, accountability, and fairness in AI systems.

- o Additionally, the EU has developed **Ethics Guidelines for Trustworthy AI**, which emphasize the importance of ensuring that AI systems are lawful, ethical, and robust, focusing on areas such as fairness, transparency, and accountability.

2. **Organisation for Economic Co-operation and Development (OECD)**:
   - o The **OECD AI Principles** provide a global framework for AI governance, focusing on promoting AI that is inclusive, sustainable, and trustworthy. These principles emphasize the need for human-centered AI, the promotion of innovation, and the protection of fundamental rights.
   - o The OECD guidelines also address the importance of fostering collaboration between governments, industry, and civil society to ensure that AI benefits all people equitably.

3. **The United Nations (UN)**:
   - o The UN has established various initiatives to govern AI's impact on society. For example, the **UN's AI for Good Global Summit** brings together experts to discuss AI's potential to address global challenges, such as climate change, poverty, and health.

o The **UN's High-Level Panel on Digital Cooperation** explores how AI can be developed and used to promote peace, security, and human rights, aligning AI technology with the broader goals of the UN, including sustainable development.

4. **The Institute of Electrical and Electronics Engineers (IEEE)**:
   o IEEE has published **Ethically Aligned Design**, a set of guidelines that aims to ensure that AI systems are designed and implemented in ways that respect ethical principles and human values. It advocates for the incorporation of ethical considerations in the design of autonomous systems and AI applications.

Real-World Example: AI Ethics Guidelines from Organizations like the EU and OECD

European Union (EU):

- The EU has created the **AI Act**, which classifies AI systems based on their risk level, ranging from minimal to high-risk applications. High-risk systems (e.g., in healthcare, law enforcement, or transportation) are subject to stricter regulations, including documentation, transparency, and human oversight. This regulatory framework aims to ensure that AI systems operate in a trustworthy and human-centered manner.

OECD:

- The **OECD AI Principles** promote values such as transparency, accountability, and fairness. For example, the principle of **fairness** urges that AI systems should be designed to avoid discrimination, ensuring that they are inclusive and accessible to all individuals, regardless of background. Similarly, the **transparency** principle advocates for making AI systems understandable and predictable, empowering users to make informed decisions.

Summary

In this chapter, we delved into the philosophical foundations of AI ethics, including **utilitarianism**, **deontology**, and **virtue ethics**, and how they provide a framework for responsible AI design. We explored how these ethical principles can be translated into practice, focusing on areas like transparency, fairness, and accountability in AI systems. Additionally, we examined **global AI guidelines** and policies from organizations like the EU and OECD, highlighting their efforts to regulate AI development in an ethical and responsible manner.

The chapter concluded with a look at real-world examples, such as the **EU AI Act** and **OECD AI Principles**, that provide concrete frameworks for designing ethical AI systems that prioritize human well-being and societal good.

As AI continues to evolve and permeate all aspects of life, the ethical considerations we've discussed will be essential in guiding the future of AI development and ensuring that these technologies benefit everyone, equally and justly.

CHAPTER 4

The Importance of Fairness in AI

What is Fairness in AI?

Fairness in AI is the concept of ensuring that artificial intelligence systems operate without discriminating against or favoring certain groups or individuals based on their characteristics, such as gender, race, socioeconomic status, or disability. Fairness aims to ensure that AI systems produce results that are equitable and just, without reinforcing existing societal inequalities.

As AI systems become more embedded in critical decision-making areas—such as hiring, law enforcement, healthcare, and finance—ensuring fairness is essential to prevent these systems from perpetuating or amplifying biases and inequalities.

Understanding Key Concepts:

- **Bias**: In AI, bias refers to the presence of systematic errors that favor certain outcomes over others. These biases may arise due to skewed data, biased algorithms, or unintended consequences of the way AI models are designed or deployed.
- **Equality**: Equality in AI focuses on providing equal treatment to all individuals, ensuring that no group is systematically disadvantaged or advantaged by the system. While fairness often

goes beyond simple equality, achieving equality is a key component of fair AI systems.

- **Fairness**: Fairness in AI goes beyond simply treating everyone equally. It seeks to ensure that outcomes are just, considering the context and the impact on different groups of people. It involves creating models that are free from discrimination and reflect ethical principles like equity and justice.

In practice, fairness in AI often involves making trade-offs between equality (e.g., equal representation) and equity (e.g., addressing systemic disparities). Ensuring fairness is not just a technical challenge but also a moral and societal one.

Types of Bias in AI

Bias in AI can manifest in various ways, and understanding these different types of bias is crucial to designing fair and responsible AI systems. Below are the primary types of bias that can affect AI systems:

1. **Dataset Bias**:
   - **Definition**: Dataset bias occurs when the data used to train an AI model is not representative of the real-world population or the task the model is meant to solve. This can happen if the data is skewed toward certain groups or if some groups are underrepresented.
   - **Examples**:

- **Gender Bias**: If a facial recognition model is primarily trained on images of white, male faces, it may perform poorly on images of women or people of color.
- **Racial Bias**: If an AI system is trained on historical data where certain groups have been systematically disadvantaged (e.g., marginalized racial groups), the model might inherit those prejudices and continue to make biased decisions.
  - **Impact**: The model may produce inaccurate or unfair predictions, leading to harmful outcomes for certain groups of people.

2. **Algorithmic Bias**:
   - **Definition**: Algorithmic bias arises when the algorithm or model itself introduces or amplifies bias in its predictions or decisions. Even with a well-balanced dataset, certain algorithms might inadvertently favor one outcome over another due to their design or the way they process data.
   - **Examples**:
     - **Overfitting**: If a model is overfitted to biased training data, it may become biased and perform poorly when exposed to real-world, diverse data.

- **Feature Selection Bias**: If the model relies on features that are themselves biased or reflective of historical inequalities (e.g., using ZIP codes as a proxy for socio-economic status), the algorithm may produce biased outcomes.
  - **Impact**: This can perpetuate inequality, as AI systems based on biased algorithms might amplify discriminatory patterns or practices.

3. **Feedback Bias**:
   - **Definition**: Feedback bias occurs when AI systems perpetuate existing biases over time due to feedback loops. These loops reinforce biases by continuously using biased data to make predictions, which further skews the model.
   - **Examples**:
     - **Recommendation Systems**: For example, if a content recommendation system on a streaming platform suggests popular content based on user preferences, it can create a feedback loop that amplifies the popularity of certain types of content (e.g., favoring certain genres or creators) while ignoring others.
     - **Hiring Algorithms**: If an AI-driven recruitment system is trained on historical hiring data

that has bias against certain groups (e.g., women or minority candidates), it may continue to prefer candidates from historically favored groups.

- o **Impact**: Over time, feedback bias can lead to systemic and reinforcing discrimination, making it difficult for marginalized groups to break into certain domains or industries.

How to Achieve Fairness in AI: Techniques and Best Practices

Achieving fairness in AI requires addressing the underlying biases that may arise during data collection, model development, and deployment. Below are some techniques and best practices to ensure fairness in AI systems:

1. **Data Preprocessing**:
   - o **Balanced Data**: Ensure that the data used to train AI models is representative and free from bias. This may involve collecting additional data to balance the representation of different groups or features.
   - o **Data Augmentation**: This technique involves artificially increasing the diversity of data by transforming existing data (e.g., rotating images, adding noise, or changing text) to ensure the model learns more generalized patterns.

- o **Debiasing Data**: Apply techniques like **reweighting** or **resampling** to adjust datasets and reduce the impact of biased data.
2. **Fairness Constraints**:
   - o **Constraint-based Methods**: During model training, fairness constraints can be added to the optimization process. These constraints enforce fairness by limiting the amount of bias the model can introduce. For example, ensuring that the model's decisions are independent of sensitive attributes like gender or race.
   - o **Equal Opportunity**: Ensure that models provide equal opportunities for all groups, especially in high-stakes domains like hiring, lending, or law enforcement. One method is to ensure that the true positive rate is equal across different groups.
3. **Algorithmic Transparency and Explainability**:
   - o **Model Explainability**: It is crucial to make AI models interpretable and explainable so that stakeholders can understand how decisions are being made and whether they are fair. Techniques such as **LIME** and **SHAP** can provide explanations for complex machine learning models.
   - o **Transparency in Decision-Making**: AI developers should ensure that the factors influencing model decisions are clear to

users, especially when these decisions affect people's lives.

4. **Auditing and Monitoring**:
   - ○ **Regular Audits**: Implement continuous monitoring and auditing to ensure AI systems remain fair over time. This includes identifying and addressing any biases that may emerge as new data is introduced or as the model is deployed in different environments.
   - ○ **Third-Party Audits**: Independent organizations can conduct audits to ensure that AI systems meet fairness standards, helping to build trust and accountability.

5. **Diverse Development Teams**:
   - ○ **Inclusive Design**: Involve diverse stakeholders, including people from different socio-economic backgrounds, genders, ethnicities, and expertise, to identify and address potential biases in AI systems. This ensures that a broader range of perspectives is considered during development.
   - ○ **Collaboration with Affected Communities**: Engage with the communities that AI systems will impact to understand their needs, values, and concerns. This helps ensure that the systems are designed with fairness and inclusivity in mind.

Real-World Example: Bias in Hiring Algorithms and How It Was Addressed

One of the most prominent real-world examples of bias in AI systems is in **hiring algorithms** used by companies to screen job applicants. These AI systems often rely on historical data to make decisions about who is a good candidate for a role. If the historical data is biased (e.g., if past hiring practices favored male candidates over female candidates), the AI system may replicate these biases.

Example: Amazon's Hiring Algorithm:

- In 2018, **Amazon** scrapped its internal AI tool for hiring after discovering that it was biased against women. The algorithm had been trained on resumes submitted to Amazon over a ten-year period, which were overwhelmingly from male candidates due to the tech industry's gender imbalance.
- **Outcome**: The algorithm was found to favor male candidates for technical roles because it learned patterns from the historical data where men had dominated those roles. This led to the AI system penalizing resumes that contained words like "women's," as it associated them with less qualified candidates.

Addressing the Bias:

- **Bias Detection**: Amazon's team identified the problem through testing and analysis. The system's reliance on historical data was a key factor in its biased outcomes.

- **Mitigation**: Amazon decided to abandon the tool and rework its approach to recruitment. They worked on improving data collection methods and implemented fairness audits to ensure that future AI tools used in recruitment did not favor one gender over another.
- **Long-Term Solution**: Moving forward, AI systems used for hiring at Amazon would have more stringent guidelines for fairness and would be continuously audited to prevent bias.

Key Lessons:

- **Data Quality**: Bias in hiring algorithms is often a reflection of biased data. Ensuring that the data is representative and free of historical biases is essential.
- **Transparency and Accountability**: Companies must be transparent about how their AI systems work, particularly when the systems affect people's livelihoods. Accountability structures should be in place to prevent discriminatory practices.

Summary

In this chapter, we explored the concept of **fairness in AI**, emphasizing its importance in creating AI systems that are just, equitable, and free from discrimination.

We discussed the different types of bias—**dataset bias, algorithmic bias**, and **feedback bias**—and how these can lead to unfair outcomes.

We also highlighted key techniques for achieving fairness, including **data preprocessing, fairness constraints, algorithmic transparency**, and **continuous auditing**. By following these best practices, developers can build more responsible and fair AI systems.

The chapter concluded with a real-world example of **bias in hiring algorithms**, illustrating how AI can perpetuate discrimination if not carefully designed and monitored. Amazon's experience with its biased recruitment tool provides valuable insights into how biases can arise and how they can be addressed through careful data management, transparency, and accountability.

As AI continues to be integrated into crucial decision-making processes, ensuring fairness will be one of the most significant challenges and responsibilities for AI developers, researchers, and policymakers.

CHAPTER 5

Transparency and Explainability in AI Systems

Why Transparency Matters: Building Trust and Accountability in AI

As artificial intelligence systems are increasingly involved in making decisions that impact people's lives—ranging from loan approvals to healthcare diagnoses—the need for transparency has never been greater. **Transparency** in AI refers to the ability to understand how AI systems make decisions, the factors influencing those decisions, and how they operate. Without transparency, AI systems risk being perceived as "black boxes" whose decisions are opaque and difficult to scrutinize.

Why is Transparency Crucial?

1. **Building Trust**: For AI systems to be widely adopted, users must trust that the decisions made by these systems are fair, justified, and unbiased. If users cannot understand or question the reasoning behind AI decisions, it becomes difficult to trust those decisions. Transparency helps foster this trust by providing clear insights into how the system works.
2. **Accountability**: When AI systems make mistakes or cause harm, it's essential to know who is responsible. Transparency enables the identification of potential issues in the system and ensures that there is a clear line of

accountability. This is particularly important in high-stakes applications, such as law enforcement or healthcare, where errors can have significant consequences.

3. **Ethical Responsibility**: Ethical AI requires transparency to ensure that AI systems are operating within defined moral boundaries. This includes ensuring that the system does not discriminate or perpetuate harmful biases. Transparency provides the means to assess whether these ethical guidelines are being followed and whether the system is functioning as intended.

4. **Regulatory Compliance**: Governments and organizations are increasingly implementing regulations that require AI systems to be explainable and accountable. Transparency is often a key aspect of these regulations, and organizations that use AI must ensure that their systems comply with legal requirements.

Explainable AI (XAI): Making AI Decisions Understandable to Humans

Explainable AI (XAI) refers to methods and techniques used to make the behavior of AI systems more understandable to humans. While AI systems, particularly deep learning models, have shown exceptional performance, they are often considered "black boxes" because their decision-making processes are not immediately clear to users. XAI seeks to bridge this gap by providing interpretable explanations for the decisions made by AI models.

1. **The Need for Explainability**:
   o **Complexity of AI Models**: Many modern AI models, especially deep learning and neural networks, are highly complex and contain millions of parameters. While these models achieve impressive performance, their inner workings are often difficult to understand, even for AI experts. This lack of explainability makes it challenging to trust or audit their decisions.
   o **User Trust and Adoption**: In applications like healthcare, finance, and criminal justice, users need to understand how decisions are made. For example, if an AI model is used to recommend treatment for a patient, it is important for doctors and patients to understand why a particular recommendation was made. The lack of explanation can hinder adoption and acceptance.
2. **The Goal of XAI**:
   o **Transparency in Decision Making**: XAI seeks to provide explanations that are accessible, understandable, and actionable, ensuring that users can grasp the reasoning behind AI decisions. This can help stakeholders make informed decisions, validate outcomes, and correct errors when necessary.
   o **Accountability and Ethical Responsibility**: With XAI, developers and organizations can ensure that AI

models are making ethical and fair decisions. Transparent models can be audited and adjusted if biases or ethical concerns are identified.

Techniques for Explainability: LIME, SHAP, Model Interpretability

There are several key techniques for making AI models more interpretable and explainable. These techniques help break down complex AI models into understandable components that can be communicated to non-experts, stakeholders, or end-users.

1. **LIME (Local Interpretable Model-agnostic Explanations)**:
   o **How LIME Works**: LIME is a technique that explains the predictions of machine learning models by approximating them with simpler, interpretable models. LIME works by creating a local approximation of the model around a particular prediction, using interpretable models (e.g., linear regression or decision trees) to explain the decision made by the complex model.
   o **Use Case**: LIME is useful when working with models that are not inherently interpretable, like deep learning models or ensemble methods. It provides a local explanation that is specific to the prediction made, allowing users to

understand why a particular decision was reached.

Example: If an AI system predicts whether a loan application should be approved, LIME could help explain the decision by showing which factors (e.g., income, credit score, loan amount) were most influential in the prediction for that specific applicant.

2. **SHAP (SHapley Additive exPlanations)**:
   o **How SHAP Works**: SHAP is a method based on cooperative game theory, where the contribution of each feature to the prediction is determined by calculating the Shapley values. These values represent the average contribution of a feature across all possible combinations of features, ensuring a fair and consistent measure of feature importance.
   o **Use Case**: SHAP is useful for providing global and local explanations. It can be used to explain the importance of individual features across all predictions or provide detailed, instance-specific explanations of model decisions.

Example: If an AI model used to predict medical outcomes makes a recommendation, SHAP could provide an explanation of which features (e.g., age, medical history, test results) contributed the most to the model's decision for a specific patient.

3. **Model Interpretability**:
   o **Definition**: Model interpretability refers to the degree to which a human can understand the cause of a decision made by an AI system. While deep learning models are often seen as opaque, some models are inherently more interpretable, such as decision trees, linear regression, or rule-based systems.
   o **Improving Interpretability**: For complex models, developers may employ techniques such as simplifying the model (e.g., reducing the number of layers in deep neural networks) or using interpretable surrogate models to approximate predictions.

   Example: Decision trees are a simple model that are inherently interpretable because they provide clear rules (e.g., "if income > $50k, then approve loan"). For more complex models like random forests, which aggregate multiple decision trees, interpretability methods like LIME or SHAP can be used to provide transparency.

Real-World Example: Using XAI in Credit Scoring Models

Credit scoring systems are widely used in financial services to determine whether a person is eligible for a loan, credit card, or mortgage. AI-driven credit scoring models have gained popularity for their ability to make quick, data-driven decisions. However, these systems can be complex, and customers or financial institutions may struggle to understand why a particular decision was made. This lack of transparency can lead to concerns about fairness, bias, and accountability.

Example: Consider an AI model used by a bank to determine whether an applicant should be approved for a loan. If the model denies a loan, it's crucial for both the applicant and the bank to understand why the decision was made, especially if the applicant feels that the decision was unfair or incorrect.

Using XAI in Credit Scoring:

1. **LIME for Local Explanations**: The bank could use LIME to provide local explanations for each loan decision. If an applicant is denied a loan, LIME could show which features (e.g., credit score, income, debt-to-income ratio) were most influential in the model's decision for that specific applicant.
2. **SHAP for Global and Local Explanations**: SHAP values could be used to provide a comprehensive understanding of how each feature affects the decision-making process. This could be presented to the applicant as a breakdown of how their credit score, income, and debt influenced the outcome. For the bank, SHAP can offer insights into the most important factors driving the overall loan approval decisions, helping the bank fine-tune its model for fairness and accuracy.

Challenges and Ethical Considerations:

- **Bias**: If the model is trained on historical data that reflects past inequalities (e.g., higher denial rates for certain demographic groups), it may perpetuate those biases. XAI techniques like LIME and SHAP can help identify if certain groups are being unfairly disadvantaged and provide transparency into the factors influencing these outcomes.
- **Accountability**: By using XAI, the bank can ensure that its decisions are explainable and accountable. If an applicant contests a loan decision, the bank can provide clear and understandable reasons behind the decision, improving trust in the system.
- **Fairness**: XAI can be used to ensure that the AI model is treating all applicants fairly. By explaining how decisions are made, the bank can ensure that no group is being unfairly penalized or overlooked, and can adjust the model if any fairness issues arise.

Summary

In this chapter, we explored the importance of **transparency** and **explainability** in AI systems, focusing on how they help build trust and accountability. We introduced **Explainable AI (XAI)**, a field dedicated to making AI decisions understandable to humans, and discussed the techniques used for model explainability, such as **LIME**, **SHAP**, and **model interpretability**.

We also examined a **real-world example** of how XAI is applied in **credit scoring models** to provide clear, understandable explanations for loan decisions. By using XAI techniques, financial institutions can ensure that their AI-driven decisions are transparent, fair, and accountable, improving trust among customers and stakeholders.

As AI continues to play a significant role in critical decision-making, ensuring transparency and explainability will be crucial in making these systems ethical, reliable, and acceptable to users.

This chapter sets the foundation for understanding the essential role of transparency and explainability in AI systems. It emphasizes that for AI to be trusted, especially in high-stakes areas like finance, healthcare, and criminal justice, its decisions must be clear, understandable, and accountable.

CHAPTER 6

Privacy and Data Security in AI Design

The Role of Data in AI: Data as the Lifeblood of AI

Data is fundamental to the functioning of artificial intelligence. AI models, particularly machine learning and deep learning systems, rely on large volumes of data to learn, adapt, and make predictions. In fact, data is often referred to as the "lifeblood" of AI, as it fuels the algorithms that power decision-making and automation in systems ranging from facial recognition to predictive analytics.

Why Data is Crucial in AI:

1. **Learning from Data**: Machine learning algorithms depend on data to identify patterns, make predictions, and improve over time. The more diverse, representative, and high-quality the data, the more effective the AI system will be at achieving its intended outcomes.
2. **Model Training**: AI models are trained on vast datasets, which allow the model to generalize to new data. The accuracy and effectiveness of AI systems are directly tied to the quantity and quality of the data they are trained on.
3. **Improving Accuracy**: As AI systems are exposed to more data, they can continually refine their performance, learning from past mistakes and adapting to new scenarios. This ongoing

learning process is key to the continuous improvement of AI models.

4. **Data as a Competitive Advantage**: In many industries, data is becoming one of the most valuable assets. Companies that collect and utilize vast amounts of data can gain a significant edge over competitors, using AI to personalize customer experiences, optimize operations, and create innovative products and services.

However, while data is essential for AI, it also presents significant ethical and privacy concerns, which we'll explore in the following sections.

Ethical Concerns with Data: Privacy, Consent, and Data Ownership

As AI systems increasingly rely on personal and sensitive data, several key ethical concerns must be addressed to ensure that these systems respect individual rights and societal norms. These concerns are centered around **privacy**, **consent**, and **data ownership**.

1. **Privacy**:
    o **Data Privacy**: Data privacy refers to the right of individuals to control how their personal data is collected, stored, and shared. AI systems often require vast amounts of data, which can include sensitive information such as health records, financial transactions, and personal preferences.

- o **Risks to Privacy**: AI systems that collect and process personal data may inadvertently expose this data to unauthorized access, misuse, or surveillance. For example, the data collected by AI-driven apps or devices could be used in ways that individuals did not explicitly agree to, such as selling the data to third parties or using it for invasive advertising.

2. **Consent**:
   - o **Informed Consent**: Informed consent refers to the process of ensuring that individuals are fully aware of what data is being collected, how it will be used, and the potential risks associated with the use of their data. Consent should be freely given, specific, informed, and unambiguous.
   - o **Challenges in AI**: AI systems may involve the collection of data from numerous sources (e.g., social media, sensors, online activities) without explicit consent from individuals. Users may not always be fully aware of the extent to which their data is being used or how it is being processed by AI systems.

3. **Data Ownership**:
   - o **Who Owns the Data?**: Determining who owns the data used to train AI systems is a critical issue. In many cases, data is collected by companies, which then own and control the data. However,

individuals whose data is collected often do not have clear ownership or control over how their data is used.

o **Data Sovereignty**: Data sovereignty refers to the legal and ethical principle that data should be subject to the laws and regulations of the country in which it is collected. As data crosses borders, issues of jurisdiction and international law complicate matters, especially when it comes to sensitive data like personal health or financial information.

Addressing these concerns is crucial for creating AI systems that respect privacy rights, protect individuals from exploitation, and ensure that data is used ethically and transparently.

Techniques to Ensure Privacy: Differential Privacy, Federated Learning

As AI systems become more pervasive, ensuring data privacy is essential to build trust and protect individuals' rights. Several techniques have been developed to address privacy concerns in AI design, allowing systems to make use of data without compromising privacy.

1. **Differential Privacy**:
   o **What is Differential Privacy?**: Differential privacy is a technique that allows organizations to collect and analyze data without exposing individual

data points. The goal is to provide statistical insights from the data while ensuring that the privacy of any individual within the dataset is protected.

- **How It Works**: Differential privacy involves adding "noise" to the data in such a way that the data remains useful for analysis but does not reveal specific information about any individual. For example, when analyzing survey data, random noise can be added to responses, making it impossible to trace specific responses back to an individual while still enabling useful analysis.
- **Benefits**: Differential privacy ensures that the data used in AI models cannot be traced back to any specific individual, providing a strong layer of privacy protection.
- **Use Cases**: Differential privacy is used in applications like data analytics for large organizations, where aggregate insights are needed but individual privacy must be maintained. For example, Apple uses differential privacy to collect data on user behavior while ensuring that no single user's data can be identified.

2. **Federated Learning**:
   - **What is Federated Learning?**: Federated learning is a decentralized approach to training AI models. Rather than collecting all data in one central location, federated learning allows data to

remain on users' devices (e.g., smartphones, IoT devices), and only model updates are shared.

- o **How It Works**: In federated learning, a global model is trained across many devices without needing to move the raw data to a central server. Each device trains a local model on its data and shares the updates with the central server, which aggregates them to improve the global model.

- o **Benefits**: Federated learning ensures that sensitive data stays on users' devices, thus reducing privacy risks. It also enables AI systems to be trained on diverse, distributed datasets while minimizing the risk of data breaches or misuse.

- o **Use Cases**: Federated learning is particularly useful in applications where data is sensitive or distributed, such as mobile applications (e.g., predictive text, health apps) or IoT systems (e.g., smart home devices).

By incorporating these privacy-enhancing techniques into AI design, developers can mitigate the risks associated with data collection and processing, ensuring that AI systems respect privacy while still delivering powerful insights.

Real-World Example: Data Privacy Concerns in Facial Recognition Technology

Facial recognition technology has become a widely used AI application, deployed in areas such as security, retail, law enforcement, and personal devices. While it offers significant benefits—such as enhancing security and improving user experiences—it also raises significant privacy concerns.

1. **Privacy Risks in Facial Recognition**:
   o **Invasive Surveillance**: One of the most concerning privacy issues with facial recognition technology is its potential for mass surveillance. Governments and private companies can use facial recognition to track individuals without their consent, raising concerns about the erosion of privacy rights.
   o **Data Security**: The data used for facial recognition (i.e., biometric data) is highly sensitive. If breached, it can be used for malicious purposes, such as identity theft or impersonation. Additionally, facial recognition systems may be vulnerable to misuse, such as being used to track individuals without their knowledge.
   o **Unfair Bias**: Studies have shown that facial recognition systems are more likely to misidentify people of color, women, and younger individuals, leading to biased outcomes. This bias can lead to

wrongful accusations, profiling, and discrimination.

2. **Addressing Privacy Concerns**:
   - **Regulation and Accountability**: Various jurisdictions have introduced regulations to govern the use of facial recognition technology. For instance, the **European Union** has established strict data protection laws under the **General Data Protection Regulation (GDPR)**, which impose restrictions on the use of biometric data and facial recognition technology.
   - **Transparency and Consent**: To address privacy concerns, companies that use facial recognition must be transparent about how the technology works and obtain informed consent from individuals. Users should be made aware of how their biometric data is collected, stored, and used, and they should have the ability to opt out.
   - **Bias Mitigation**: AI developers working on facial recognition systems must take steps to reduce bias in their models, ensuring that the technology works fairly and accurately across all demographic groups.

Example: In 2019, **IBM** and **Microsoft** paused the sale of their facial recognition software to law enforcement agencies, citing concerns about potential misuse and racial bias. This move reflects the growing recognition of the ethical and privacy concerns surrounding facial recognition technology and the need for responsible deployment.

Summary

In this chapter, we examined the role of **data** in AI systems, highlighting its centrality in powering machine learning models. We discussed the **ethical concerns** related to data, including **privacy**, **consent**, and **data ownership**, and explored techniques for ensuring **privacy** in AI systems, such as **differential privacy** and **federated learning**. These techniques help mitigate privacy risks while maintaining the usefulness of AI models.

We also discussed a **real-world example** of **data privacy concerns** in **facial recognition technology**, illustrating the challenges of balancing innovation with privacy protection. As AI systems increasingly rely on personal data, it is essential that privacy is protected and ethical guidelines are followed to ensure that AI technologies are used responsibly.

With the growing adoption of AI, it is crucial for developers to prioritize data privacy, safeguard individual rights, and create systems that are both powerful and ethical.

CHAPTER 7

Accountability in AI

Who is Responsible for AI Decisions?

As AI systems become more integrated into society, the question of accountability—who is responsible for the decisions made by AI systems—becomes increasingly important. AI systems are used in critical areas like healthcare, finance, law enforcement, and autonomous vehicles, where their decisions can have significant consequences for individuals, organizations, and society at large.

Key Questions of Accountability:

- **Who is responsible when an AI system makes a mistake?** When an AI system produces incorrect or harmful results, such as denying a loan, misdiagnosing a medical condition, or causing an accident, who should be held accountable? Is it the developer, the organization that deployed the system, or the AI itself?
- **Can AI systems be held accountable?** While AI systems are capable of making decisions, they are still tools created and operated by humans. Thus, the accountability for AI decisions lies with humans—whether it is the AI developers, the organizations using the AI, or the users of AI systems.
- **Shared Accountability**: Accountability in AI may involve shared responsibility across

multiple stakeholders, including developers, data scientists, business leaders, and policymakers. Developers must ensure that AI systems are designed to be safe, fair, and ethical, while organizations must ensure that the systems they deploy align with ethical standards and comply with legal regulations.

Establishing clear lines of accountability is crucial to ensure that AI systems are used responsibly and that individuals or entities can be held liable for negative outcomes.

Legal and Ethical Accountability: Laws and Regulations Governing AI

As AI systems evolve, so too do the laws and regulations that govern their use. Governments, international bodies, and organizations are introducing laws and frameworks to ensure that AI systems are used in ways that are transparent, fair, and aligned with ethical principles.

1. **Laws and Regulations**:
   - **General Data Protection Regulation (GDPR)**: One of the most well-known pieces of legislation addressing AI and data privacy is the European Union's **GDPR**. It includes provisions related to AI, especially concerning data processing, the right to explanation (for decisions made by automated systems), and data subject rights. Under the GDPR,

individuals have the right to know how their data is being used and to challenge automated decisions made by AI systems.

- o **The AI Act (EU)**: The European Union is working on the **Artificial Intelligence Act**, which aims to regulate AI in a way that balances innovation with ethical standards and societal concerns. The AI Act categorizes AI systems by risk level (e.g., minimal, high, or unacceptable risk) and introduces stricter regulations for high-risk systems, such as those used in healthcare, law enforcement, and transport.
- o **AI Ethics Guidelines**: In addition to regulatory frameworks, governments and organizations have developed ethical guidelines for AI. The **OECD AI Principles**, for example, advocate for transparent, accountable, and fair AI systems that benefit society. These principles emphasize that AI systems should be human-centric, promoting inclusivity, accountability, and fairness.

2. **Ethical Accountability**:
   - o Beyond legal frameworks, AI developers and organizations must also adhere to ethical standards that go beyond the letter of the law. These ethical standards often emphasize values such as fairness, transparency, privacy, and respect for human rights. Ethical accountability ensures that AI technologies are not just

compliant with laws but also align with broader societal values.

- ○ **Ethical Audits and Impact Assessments**: To ensure that AI systems meet ethical standards, organizations can implement ethical audits and impact assessments to evaluate the social, economic, and environmental implications of AI systems.

Challenges in Legal and Ethical Accountability:

- **Jurisdiction**: AI systems often operate across borders, complicating the enforcement of laws and regulations. For example, data used by AI systems may be stored in one country, while the system is deployed and operated in another. This raises questions about whose laws apply and how accountability can be established.
- **Complexity and Autonomy**: AI systems are often complex, with deep learning models that make decisions based on patterns in vast datasets. This complexity can make it difficult to trace exactly how decisions are made, posing challenges for accountability.

Frameworks for Accountability: AI Audits, Impact Assessments

As AI technologies become more advanced, organizations need frameworks for evaluating and ensuring accountability. Two key tools for this are **AI audits** and **impact assessments**.

1. **AI Audits**:
   - **What is an AI Audit?**: An AI audit is a comprehensive review of an AI system to ensure that it is functioning as intended and adheres to ethical standards. AI audits typically assess the fairness, transparency, safety, and performance of AI systems. Audits can be conducted internally or by third-party organizations that specialize in AI governance and ethics.
   - **The Audit Process**:
     - **Data Review**: An audit includes reviewing the data used by the AI system to identify potential biases or gaps.
     - **Model Evaluation**: The models are tested for fairness, transparency, and performance, ensuring that they meet ethical and regulatory standards.
     - **Outcome Analysis**: Auditors assess the impact of the system's decisions, looking at both intended and unintended consequences, particularly on vulnerable groups.
     - **Recommendations**: Based on the audit, recommendations are provided to improve the AI system's fairness, transparency, and accountability.

Example: In 2018, **Google** introduced an internal **AI ethics review board** to audit its AI systems and ensure that they comply with ethical guidelines. Such audits are vital for ensuring AI systems align with both legal requirements and moral principles.

2. **Impact Assessments**:
   o **What is an AI Impact Assessment?**: An AI impact assessment is a systematic process used to evaluate the potential social, economic, environmental, and ethical impacts of deploying an AI system. This process helps identify and mitigate risks that AI systems could pose to individuals or society.
   o **Types of Impact Assessments**:
      ▪ **Ethical Impact Assessment**: Evaluates the ethical implications of AI systems, such as fairness, privacy, and transparency.
      ▪ **Socioeconomic Impact Assessment**: Assesses how AI systems might affect employment, social inequality, and community well-being.
      ▪ **Environmental Impact Assessment**: Analyzes how AI technologies impact the environment, particularly in terms of energy consumption and sustainability.

- **When to Conduct Impact Assessments**: AI impact assessments should be conducted before deploying a new AI system, during system development, and periodically after deployment to ensure continued accountability.

Example: In the European Union, the **AI Act** includes provisions requiring high-risk AI systems to undergo impact assessments. For example, AI used in healthcare would be assessed for both ethical and practical impacts before being deployed to ensure patient safety and equity.

Real-World Example: Accountability in Autonomous Vehicles

Autonomous vehicles (AVs) are one of the most prominent and controversial examples of AI systems where accountability plays a crucial role. AVs use AI to navigate roads, make decisions in traffic, and respond to unexpected events. However, if an autonomous vehicle causes an accident or harm, questions arise about who is responsible.

Who is Accountable?

1. **Manufacturer Responsibility**: The manufacturer of the AV is typically held responsible for the system's design, performance, and safety. Manufacturers are responsible for ensuring that their vehicles meet

safety standards and are programmed to avoid accidents whenever possible.

2. **Software Developers**: The developers who design the AI software that controls the vehicle's decision-making processes are also accountable. If a software bug or flaw causes an accident, they could be held liable.

3. **Vehicle Owner**: In some cases, the vehicle owner may share responsibility, especially if they override or interfere with the autonomous system's decisions.

4. **Regulators**: Governments and regulators also play a role in ensuring that autonomous vehicles meet ethical and safety standards. They may set guidelines and standards for AI systems used in AVs, ensuring that manufacturers comply with legal requirements.

Case Study: Uber's Self-Driving Car Fatality:

- In 2018, an autonomous vehicle developed by Uber struck and killed a pedestrian in Arizona. This incident raised significant questions about the accountability of AVs. Investigations revealed that the vehicle's AI system failed to recognize the pedestrian in time, and the safety driver did not intervene quickly enough.

- **Outcome**: Uber paused its self-driving car testing after the incident, and the company faced scrutiny over its safety practices and the accountability of its AI system. The incident led to calls for stricter regulations and oversight of autonomous vehicle development.

Key Lessons:

- **Clear Accountability**: In the case of autonomous vehicles, clear lines of accountability must be established between manufacturers, developers, vehicle owners, and regulators. The legal and ethical responsibility for AI-driven decisions should be transparent to ensure justice when something goes wrong.
- **AI Safety and Ethics**: AVs must be designed to meet the highest safety standards, and ethical considerations, such as the potential for accidents and how AI should make decisions in crisis situations (e.g., the "trolley problem"), must be addressed early in development.
- **Regulation and Oversight**: Autonomous vehicles require robust regulations to ensure that AI systems are held to ethical standards, particularly in terms of safety, fairness, and accountability.

Summary

In this chapter, we explored the concept of **accountability** in AI systems, addressing the key question of who is responsible for AI decisions. We discussed the importance of **legal** and **ethical accountability**, and examined existing laws, frameworks, and regulations governing AI, such as the EU's **AI Act** and the **GDPR**.

We also introduced tools for ensuring accountability in AI, including **AI audits** and **impact assessments**, which help organizations evaluate the ethical, social, and legal impacts of AI systems before deployment.

Finally, we provided a **real-world example** of accountability in **autonomous vehicles**, demonstrating the importance of establishing clear responsibility and oversight for AI-driven decisions, especially in high-stakes scenarios where public safety is involved.

As AI continues to grow in influence, establishing accountability frameworks and ensuring responsible AI practices will be crucial in building trust, protecting individuals, and ensuring ethical AI deployment.

CHAPTER 8

Avoiding Harm and Unintended Consequences

Ethical AI Design: Minimizing Harm in AI Systems

Ethical AI design focuses on ensuring that AI systems are developed and deployed in ways that minimize harm and avoid negative consequences for individuals, communities, and society as a whole. When designing AI systems, it is essential to consider the potential risks and ensure that the technology works in a way that benefits all stakeholders while safeguarding against misuse, discrimination, and harm.

Key Principles of Ethical AI Design:

1. **Do No Harm**: One of the fundamental principles in ethical AI design is ensuring that AI systems do not cause harm, either intentionally or unintentionally. This includes minimizing physical harm, psychological harm, and harm to societal structures and fairness.
2. **Beneficence**: Ethical AI should contribute positively to society by improving people's lives. For instance, AI in healthcare can improve diagnoses, but it must also be designed to ensure that it serves all populations fairly and without bias.
3. **Non-maleficence**: Beyond simply avoiding harm, AI systems must be built to prevent any kind of negative impact. This could include ensuring that AI doesn't exacerbate inequalities,

violate privacy, or result in undesirable outcomes.

4. **Informed Decision-Making**: It is crucial that stakeholders involved in AI development understand the potential risks and benefits. Developers must anticipate how the AI will function and identify possible unintended consequences before deployment.

AI systems, particularly those that make decisions affecting people, should be tested for various scenarios, including worst-case outcomes. The goal is to foresee and design around potential harms by incorporating safety measures, ethical guidelines, and checks and balances throughout the development process.

Risk Assessment in AI Development: Identifying and Mitigating Risks

A critical aspect of ethical AI development is conducting comprehensive **risk assessments** to identify, evaluate, and mitigate risks associated with AI systems. Risk assessments should be conducted throughout the AI lifecycle, from data collection to model deployment and beyond.

1. **Identifying Risks**:
   o **Data Risks**: The data used to train AI models may carry inherent risks, such as biases, inaccuracies, or lack of representativeness. For example, if an AI model is trained on biased data, it may

make unfair decisions that disproportionately affect certain groups.

- o **Algorithmic Risks**: AI algorithms can introduce risks through unintended behaviors, such as reinforcing existing inequalities, amplifying harmful stereotypes, or failing in unanticipated ways (e.g., a self-driving car making incorrect decisions in complex traffic scenarios).
- o **Operational Risks**: Operational risks involve risks that arise when the AI system is deployed in real-world settings. This could include system failures, poor performance in unexpected scenarios, or security vulnerabilities that expose sensitive data to breaches.

2. **Mitigating Risks**:
- o **Bias Mitigation**: One of the most common risks in AI is bias, which can lead to discriminatory outcomes. Techniques such as fairness constraints, data augmentation, and regular audits should be implemented to ensure that the AI system performs fairly for all groups.
- o **Model Validation**: Extensive testing and validation of AI models are essential for ensuring they behave as expected. Developers should test models across diverse datasets and edge cases to ensure that they generalize well and don't introduce harmful behaviors.

- o **Continuous Monitoring**: AI systems should be continuously monitored for performance and ethical concerns after deployment. This includes tracking how the model performs in real-world applications and ensuring that any potential risks are flagged and mitigated in a timely manner.
3. **Proactive Risk Management**:
   - o **Risk Scenarios**: AI developers should think proactively about the various ways their systems could fail or cause harm. This includes considering the worst-case scenarios and developing mechanisms to prevent or respond to them.
   - o **Collaborative Risk Mitigation**: Collaboration between developers, ethicists, legal experts, and affected communities is essential to ensure that AI systems are designed with a holistic understanding of potential risks.

How to Handle Unintended Outcomes: Designing for Safety

Despite careful planning, AI systems may still produce unintended outcomes. Whether due to unforeseen circumstances or inherent complexities, it's essential to have mechanisms in place to **design for safety** and mitigate these outcomes.

1. **Fail-Safes and Safeguards**:

- **Human-in-the-Loop**: Incorporating human oversight into AI systems can help mitigate unintended outcomes. A human-in-the-loop (HITL) approach allows human intervention when the AI system reaches a decision point that may be controversial, risky, or uncertain. For example, an AI system used in healthcare could suggest a treatment, but a doctor would ultimately make the final decision.
- **Fail-Safe Mechanisms**: AI systems, especially those in critical applications like autonomous vehicles or industrial machinery, should be equipped with fail-safe mechanisms that activate if something goes wrong. These mechanisms can take the system offline or switch it to a safe state to prevent harm.

2. **Error Handling and Adaptation**:
   - **Self-Correction**: In some cases, AI systems may be designed to learn from their mistakes and self-correct over time. This is particularly relevant for AI systems that operate in dynamic environments (e.g., recommendation systems or adaptive learning platforms).
   - **Adaptive Behavior**: AI systems should be designed to adapt to new information or unforeseen situations. For instance, an AI system deployed in a new geographic location should be able to adapt its predictions based on local factors, such as

cultural differences or infrastructure variations.

3. **Ethical Design Choices**:
   o **Value Alignment**: AI systems must be designed to align with human values. This involves explicitly programming ethical considerations into the design, ensuring that systems behave in ways that are consistent with the values of the society in which they operate.
   o **Contingency Planning**: Anticipating potential failures or harmful outcomes should be part of the AI design process. For example, developers should plan for situations where an autonomous vehicle must make life-and-death decisions or how a financial AI system should handle extreme economic conditions.

Real-World Example: Harm Caused by Biased Predictive Policing Systems

Predictive policing uses AI algorithms to analyze crime data and predict where future crimes are likely to occur. These systems are intended to help law enforcement agencies allocate resources more effectively and reduce crime. However, they can also introduce significant harm when they are not designed and implemented responsibly.

1. **The Problem with Predictive Policing**:
   o **Bias in Crime Data**: Predictive policing systems often rely on historical crime

data, which can be biased due to historical over-policing of certain communities, particularly minority neighborhoods. As a result, these systems may reinforce existing biases, directing police resources disproportionately to already over-policed areas, which can lead to further harassment and discrimination.

- o **Amplifying Disparities**: Studies have shown that predictive policing tools often target minority communities, exacerbating existing inequalities. For example, when an AI system is trained on biased data that over-represents arrests in certain neighborhoods, it may generate predictions that encourage more policing in those same areas, regardless of the actual likelihood of crime.

2. **Addressing the Harm**:
   - o **Bias Detection and Correction**: To address the harms caused by biased predictive policing, developers must implement techniques to detect and correct bias in the data used to train these systems. This includes analyzing the historical data for patterns of racial bias and ensuring that the model does not unfairly target specific communities.
   - o **Transparency and Accountability**: Law enforcement agencies must be transparent about how predictive policing systems are used and the data they rely on. Community input and oversight are

critical to ensure that these systems do not perpetuate harmful practices or violate individuals' rights.

○ **Ongoing Monitoring and Evaluation**: Continuous monitoring of predictive policing systems is necessary to identify unintended consequences, such as increased surveillance of minority communities. Agencies must assess the social impact of these systems and make adjustments as needed to ensure they serve the public fairly.

Example: The COMPAS Algorithm: One widely used tool in predictive policing is the **COMPAS (Correctional Offender Management Profiling for Alternative Sanctions)** algorithm. The system is used to assess the likelihood of an individual reoffending and is often employed in sentencing and parole decisions. However, investigations revealed that COMPAS had significant racial biases, with the system being more likely to falsely label Black defendants as high risk for reoffending compared to White defendants. This led to calls for greater transparency, fairness, and oversight in predictive tools used in criminal justice.

Summary

In this chapter, we discussed the importance of **minimizing harm** and avoiding **unintended consequences** in AI systems. We explored the role of **ethical AI design** in ensuring that AI systems are developed responsibly and avoid causing harm to individuals and society. Key strategies for minimizing harm include **risk assessments**, **bias mitigation**, and **continuous monitoring**.

We also covered techniques for **designing for safety**, such as **human-in-the-loop systems** and **fail-safe mechanisms**, which help AI systems respond to unexpected situations and mitigate potential risks.

The chapter concluded with a **real-world example** of **harm caused by biased predictive policing systems**, illustrating how AI systems can unintentionally perpetuate discrimination and inequality. By addressing these issues through transparency, accountability, and bias correction, we can ensure that AI systems contribute positively to society while minimizing harmful impacts.

As AI systems continue to play a more significant role in decision-making, it is essential for developers, policymakers, and stakeholders to prioritize ethical design and safety to ensure that AI serves humanity's best interests.

CHAPTER 9

Autonomy vs. Control in AI

Human-AI Collaboration: The Balance Between AI Decision-Making and Human Oversight

The development of AI systems that can make decisions independently has sparked an ongoing debate about the right balance between **AI autonomy** and **human control**. AI systems, particularly in fields like healthcare, law enforcement, transportation, and defense, have the potential to perform tasks faster, more accurately, and more efficiently than humans. However, the question remains: **How much decision-making power should AI systems have, and where do we draw the line between autonomy and human oversight?**

Human-AI Collaboration refers to a model where AI systems assist humans in decision-making, providing recommendations, predictions, and insights, but the final decision is made by a human. This collaboration leverages the strengths of both parties:

- **AI's Strengths**: AI systems can analyze large datasets, detect patterns, and make real-time decisions that would be difficult or impossible for humans to do manually. AI can also handle repetitive or mundane tasks, allowing humans to focus on more strategic, creative, or interpersonal work.

- **Human Strengths**: Humans provide intuition, emotional intelligence, and moral judgment that AI systems are not capable of. In complex or high-stakes situations, human oversight ensures that AI systems remain aligned with ethical standards, societal values, and legal frameworks.

Finding the Right Balance:

1. **Augmentation vs. Replacement**: AI should augment human decision-making rather than replace it entirely. By working together, AI and humans can enhance decision outcomes and improve efficiency while preserving human oversight.
2. **Accountability**: Humans should always maintain ultimate responsibility for decisions made by AI systems, especially when those decisions have significant consequences for people's lives. This is particularly important in fields like healthcare and criminal justice, where AI's recommendations can directly affect individuals' well-being or freedoms.

Examples of Human-AI Collaboration:

- **Healthcare**: AI systems may assist doctors by analyzing medical images, identifying patterns in patient data, and suggesting possible diagnoses. However, the final decision on diagnosis and treatment should remain in the hands of a qualified healthcare professional.

- **Autonomous Vehicles**: In autonomous vehicles, AI can handle navigation, obstacle detection, and traffic management, but human drivers must retain the ability to take control if the AI system encounters a complex situation it cannot handle.

The Dangers of Autonomous Systems: Risks of Full Autonomy in Critical Sectors

While autonomy in AI has the potential to drive significant advancements, particularly in industries like transportation, defense, and healthcare, **full autonomy**—where AI systems make decisions without human intervention—introduces substantial risks, particularly in **high-stakes applications**. Autonomous systems, while capable of performing tasks independently, can also fail in unpredictable ways, especially in complex or unforeseen situations.

Risks of Full Autonomy:

1. **Lack of Accountability**: In fully autonomous systems, it can be difficult to assign responsibility when something goes wrong. If an autonomous vehicle causes an accident, for example, it might be unclear who is to blame: the vehicle manufacturer, the software developer, or the vehicle owner? Without human oversight, accountability becomes murky.
2. **Unintended Consequences**: Autonomous systems may make decisions based on logic or data that humans might find morally or ethically troubling. AI algorithms, particularly those in

complex systems like self-driving cars or military drones, may face scenarios where no clear moral or ethical decision can be made. For example, in a situation where a vehicle must decide whom to harm in order to avoid a larger disaster, it may face a moral dilemma that AI isn't prepared to handle effectively.

3. **Vulnerability to Errors**: AI systems are not infallible. In complex, real-world scenarios, even well-trained AI systems can make mistakes, sometimes with severe consequences. AI systems that operate without human oversight may fail to account for rare but critical events, such as sudden changes in the environment or abnormal patterns that they haven't encountered before.

4. **Security Risks**: Fully autonomous systems may be vulnerable to hacking or cyberattacks. If an AI system controlling a critical infrastructure (like a power grid or self-driving car) is hacked, it could result in catastrophic outcomes. Without human intervention or oversight, it can be difficult to detect or mitigate these attacks.

Examples of Autonomous Systems in Critical Sectors:

- **Autonomous Vehicles**: While many car manufacturers are testing self-driving cars, fully autonomous vehicles that operate without human drivers are still rare. A tragic example of the risks of full autonomy occurred in 2018, when an autonomous Uber vehicle struck and killed a pedestrian. While the vehicle was designed to navigate without a human driver, human oversight was lacking at critical moments, leading to the fatal accident.

- **Healthcare**: In healthcare, AI systems that independently make diagnostic decisions could be risky. For example, a fully autonomous AI system in a hospital that decides which patients should receive a life-saving treatment could fail to recognize rare conditions or nuanced medical situations that a human doctor might catch.

Ensuring Human Control: Keeping Humans in the Loop

To mitigate the risks associated with full autonomy, it is crucial to maintain **human control** over AI systems, especially in high-stakes and critical sectors. This ensures that AI remains a tool to assist human decision-making rather than replace it entirely.

Key Approaches to Ensure Human Control:

1. **Human-in-the-Loop (HITL)**: HITL refers to the concept of maintaining human oversight in AI systems. Even if AI is performing most tasks autonomously, humans must have the ability to intervene if needed. HITL systems are particularly important in situations where AI decisions could have life-altering consequences, such as in military applications, healthcare, and transportation.
    - o **Example**: In autonomous vehicles, HITL can ensure that a human driver is always

able to take control of the car if the AI system encounters a situation it cannot handle.

- o **Example**: In military drone operations, a human operator can override AI-driven targeting decisions to prevent unintended harm or collateral damage.

2. **AI Transparency and Explainability**: Ensuring that AI systems are transparent and explainable is key to maintaining human control. If AI systems are not transparent, it becomes difficult for humans to understand how the system is making decisions, which undermines trust and accountability. When AI models are explainable, humans can better understand the rationale behind the AI's decisions and make informed choices about whether to intervene or override the system.

   - o **Example**: In autonomous vehicles, explainable AI could provide real-time information to the driver about how the vehicle is making decisions, allowing them to intervene if necessary.

3. **Ethical and Legal Frameworks**: Developing ethical guidelines and legal frameworks that define when and how human intervention is required is essential for maintaining control over AI systems. These frameworks should outline the responsibilities of human operators, developers, and organizations to ensure that AI systems are used safely and ethically.

   - o **Example**: In the case of military drones, international laws and ethical frameworks, such as the **Geneva Conventions**, should define when human intervention is required to prevent unlawful targeting or excessive harm.

4. **Autonomous System Fail-Safes**: In addition to human oversight, autonomous systems should be designed with fail-safe mechanisms that allow them to safely revert to human control or enter a safe state in case of malfunction or unexpected behavior. These safeguards ensure that AI systems can still function safely and effectively, even in situations where they cannot operate autonomously.

   o **Example**: A self-driving car may include a fail-safe that brings the vehicle to a complete stop if the AI detects an error in its decision-making process or encounters an obstacle that it cannot navigate around.

Real-World Example: Autonomous Drones in Military Applications

Autonomous drones are one of the most complex and controversial examples of AI systems operating with varying degrees of autonomy. In military applications, drones are used for surveillance, reconnaissance, and targeted strikes. However, when these systems are fully autonomous, they raise significant ethical, moral, and legal concerns, particularly when it comes to the use of force and decision-making in conflict situations.

1. **The Dangers of Full Autonomy in Military Drones**:

- o **Decision-Making in Combat**: Autonomous drones used for targeted strikes must make critical decisions about who to target. In situations where a drone has to decide who poses a threat, it might misidentify individuals or fail to account for the full context of a situation, leading to civilian casualties or wrongful targeting.
- o **Accountability**: If an autonomous drone makes a decision that leads to harm or violation of international law, it is unclear who should be held accountable—the manufacturer, the software developer, the military, or the AI system itself? This lack of clarity in accountability is a key challenge in military AI systems.

2. **Ensuring Human Control**:
   - o **Human Oversight in Targeting**: In some military applications, AI systems may assist in surveillance and identifying potential targets, but human operators are required to make the final decision regarding the use of force. This is essential to ensure that autonomous systems adhere to ethical guidelines, international law, and the rules of engagement.
   - o **Example**: The U.S. military's **Reaper drone** program, which has been used for both surveillance and targeted strikes, involves human operators who make the final decision about which targets to

engage, even though AI is used to assist in identifying targets.

Challenges in Military AI:

- **Ethical Concerns**: Autonomous drones raise significant ethical concerns about delegating life-and-death decisions to machines. There is also the question of whether AI should ever be allowed to independently make decisions that result in lethal force.
- **Legal Frameworks**: International law currently does not fully address the ethical, moral, and legal implications of autonomous military systems. As AI-driven weapons become more advanced, it will be crucial to establish clear legal frameworks that define acceptable use and ensure accountability.

Summary

In this chapter, we explored the tension between **autonomy** and **control** in AI systems, particularly in critical sectors where AI decisions have significant consequences. We discussed the importance of **human-AI collaboration**, where AI systems assist human decision-making rather than replacing it, and examined the **dangers of full autonomy** in systems like autonomous vehicles and military drones.

We emphasized the need to **ensure human control** in AI systems through mechanisms like **human-in-the-loop (HITL) systems, AI transparency, ethical frameworks**, and **fail-safe mechanisms**. These measures ensure that humans remain responsible for AI decisions and can intervene when necessary to prevent harm.

Finally, we discussed a **real-world example** of **autonomous drones in military applications**, highlighting the ethical, moral, and legal concerns associated with fully autonomous systems in conflict situations. As AI continues to evolve, finding the right balance between autonomy and human control will be crucial to ensuring that AI systems operate safely, ethically, and in alignment with human values.

CHAPTER 10

AI and Discrimination

How AI Can Perpetuate Discrimination: Examples of AI Systems Reinforcing Social Inequalities

Artificial intelligence (AI) has the potential to revolutionize many aspects of society, from improving healthcare to optimizing business processes. However, AI systems are also at risk of perpetuating and amplifying existing social inequalities. This occurs because AI systems often rely on historical data, which can contain biases that reflect past discriminatory practices. When AI models are trained on biased data, they may unknowingly learn and replicate those biases in their predictions and decisions.

Examples of AI Reinforcing Social Inequalities:

1. **Hiring Algorithms**: AI systems used to screen resumes or evaluate job candidates can perpetuate gender, racial, or age-related discrimination. For example, a recruitment algorithm trained on past hiring data from a predominantly male workforce might develop a preference for male candidates, even if that bias is not intentional. Similarly, AI systems trained on biased historical data may disadvantage minority or underrepresented groups.

2. **Criminal Justice**: Predictive policing algorithms and risk assessment tools used in sentencing and parole decisions can reinforce

existing biases in the criminal justice system. For instance, if these systems are trained on historical arrest data, which may be biased against certain racial or ethnic groups, the AI may perpetuate these biases, leading to over-policing of certain communities and unfair sentencing outcomes.

3. **Healthcare**: AI systems used in healthcare may inadvertently disadvantage certain groups. For instance, facial recognition software used in diagnosing skin conditions may perform less accurately on darker skin tones because it was predominantly trained on lighter skin. Similarly, predictive models used in healthcare settings may be trained on data that underrepresents certain populations, leading to inaccurate diagnoses or treatment recommendations for those groups.

4. **Credit Scoring**: AI-driven credit scoring systems that use data from financial history to assess creditworthiness may be biased toward certain demographics. For example, if the data used to train the model reflects historical economic inequalities, the algorithm may unfairly penalize individuals from low-income or minority communities, limiting their access to loans and other financial services.

The Risk of Discriminatory Outcomes: AI systems can unintentionally produce discriminatory outcomes when they are trained on biased or incomplete data, or when they reinforce existing social inequalities. As AI becomes more integrated into decision-making in areas like hiring, criminal justice, healthcare, and finance, it is crucial to ensure that these systems do not disproportionately harm vulnerable or marginalized communities.

Understanding Discrimination in AI Models: Disparate Impact vs. Disparate Treatment

To understand how AI can perpetuate discrimination, it's important to distinguish between two legal and ethical concepts: **disparate impact** and **disparate treatment**.

1. **Disparate Impact**:
    o **Definition**: Disparate impact occurs when a seemingly neutral AI system disproportionately affects a certain group, even if the system was not designed to discriminate. In other words, the outcomes of the AI model result in unfairly disadvantaging one group over others, regardless of the model's intent.
    o **Example**: An AI-powered hiring tool that prioritizes candidates with higher education levels may inadvertently disadvantage candidates from lower-income backgrounds, who may not have had the same access to education opportunities. Even though the hiring tool may not intentionally discriminate based on income, its criteria may result in disparate impact against people from

disadvantaged   socio-economic backgrounds.

2. **Disparate Treatment**:
   - **Definition**: Disparate treatment occurs when AI systems explicitly treat individuals from different groups differently based on characteristics such as race, gender, or age. This form of discrimination is more direct, and involves intentional or unintentional bias in the system's design or decision-making process.
   - **Example**: A loan approval system that gives preferential treatment to male applicants over female applicants, or a facial recognition system that has higher accuracy for white faces than for people of color, is an example of disparate treatment.

In AI systems, both disparate impact and disparate treatment are critical issues. Ensuring fairness involves addressing both forms of discrimination, even if bias is not intentional.

Strategies to Prevent Discrimination: Fairness Constraints and Auditing

To mitigate the risks of discrimination in AI systems, it is essential to implement strategies that promote fairness, transparency, and accountability. These strategies help ensure that AI systems operate equitably for all groups and do not inadvertently perpetuate harmful biases.

1. **Fairness Constraints**:
   - **Definition**: Fairness constraints are guidelines or rules implemented in the training of AI models to ensure that the outcomes do not disproportionately disadvantage certain groups. These constraints can be built into the algorithm during model training or post-processing stages.
   - **Types of Fairness Constraints**:
     - **Demographic Parity**: Ensures that the AI system's outcomes are distributed equally among different groups, such as gender or race. For example, a hiring algorithm should not select candidates based on characteristics like gender, and should aim to ensure equal representation across different groups.
     - **Equalized Odds**: Ensures that the model's error rates (false positives and false negatives) are equal across groups. For example, a criminal justice risk assessment tool should not have a higher false positive rate for Black defendants compared to White defendants.
     - **Individual Fairness**: Ensures that similar individuals are treated

similarly by the AI system. For example, two applicants with similar qualifications and experiences should receive similar outcomes, regardless of demographic characteristics.

2. **Auditing and Monitoring**:
   - **Bias Audits**: Regular audits of AI systems can identify potential biases in the data, algorithms, and decision-making processes. These audits help detect when AI systems are disproportionately affecting certain groups and allow organizations to adjust the system to improve fairness.
   - **Algorithmic Transparency**: Ensuring transparency in AI models allows stakeholders to understand how decisions are being made, making it easier to detect and correct any discriminatory patterns. This transparency is essential for building trust and accountability.
   - **Continuous Monitoring**: Since AI systems can evolve over time, it's crucial to continuously monitor their performance and outcomes to ensure that they continue to operate fairly and without discrimination. Ongoing testing and adjustments should be made to ensure that biases do not emerge after deployment.

3. **Diverse Development Teams**:

- **Inclusive Design**: Involving diverse teams of developers, data scientists, and ethicists is critical in preventing bias and discrimination in AI systems. Diverse perspectives can help identify potential blind spots and ensure that the system accounts for a wide range of experiences and needs.
- **Collaboration with Affected Communities**: Engaging with the communities that will be impacted by AI systems is essential for understanding their concerns and ensuring that AI technologies serve everyone fairly. Collaborating with affected groups can lead to more inclusive and equitable AI design.

4. **Bias Detection Tools**:
   - There are several tools available that help developers identify and mitigate bias in AI models. Examples include:
     - **IBM AI Fairness 360**: A toolkit for detecting and mitigating bias in machine learning models.
     - **Google's Fairness Indicators**: A set of tools for evaluating the fairness of machine learning models in classification tasks.
     - **Microsoft's Fairlearn**: An open-source toolkit designed to assess and improve fairness in machine learning models.

Real-World Example: Discriminatory Outcomes in AI-Based Loan Approval Systems

AI-based systems are increasingly used by financial institutions to automate loan approvals. These systems often analyze a range of factors, such as income, credit history, and other financial data, to determine whether an applicant is eligible for a loan. However, there have been concerns about how these AI systems may unintentionally perpetuate discrimination against certain groups, particularly racial minorities and women.

Case Study: The Discriminatory Outcomes in Credit Scoring Models:

1. **The Problem**: Research has shown that AI-based loan approval systems can sometimes produce biased outcomes. For example, if the AI model is trained on historical data that reflects systemic discrimination against certain groups (e.g., African Americans or women), the AI may unintentionally learn to penalize applicants from these groups, even though the system itself is designed to be "neutral."

2. **Discriminatory Patterns**: If the data used to train the loan approval model contains biases (e.g., historical inequalities in income or access to credit), the AI system may "learn" these biases and use them to make decisions. For example, women or people of color might be unfairly assessed as higher-risk borrowers due to biased data reflecting historical credit inequalities,

leading to higher rejection rates or worse loan terms for these groups.

3. **Addressing the Issue**:
   o **Bias Auditing**: To address these issues, financial institutions must regularly audit their AI models to identify any bias in the decision-making process. By auditing the model's outcomes and analyzing the results across different demographic groups, organizations can identify patterns of discrimination and adjust the model accordingly.
   o **Fairness Constraints**: Financial institutions can implement fairness constraints in their AI models to ensure that demographic characteristics like gender or race do not unfairly influence loan approval decisions. These constraints could be incorporated into the training process, ensuring that the AI model treats all applicants equally and fairly, regardless of demographic factors.
   o **Transparency and Accountability**: Providing transparency about how AI models make decisions and ensuring that there is a clear process for addressing complaints can help build trust and prevent discriminatory outcomes.

Example: The 2018 Case of Apple's Credit Card: In 2018, **Apple's credit card**, which was created in partnership with Goldman Sachs, faced backlash after users reported that the AI-driven credit assessment system was offering significantly lower credit limits to women than to men, even when their financial profiles were similar. The issue raised concerns about potential gender bias in the AI system. In response, Goldman Sachs acknowledged the issue and stated they would review their practices to ensure fairness.

Summary

In this chapter, we examined how **AI can perpetuate discrimination**, particularly through biased data, algorithms, and decision-making processes. We explored the concepts of **disparate impact** and **disparate treatment**, which help to understand the various forms of discrimination that can arise in AI systems.

We also discussed **strategies to prevent discrimination** in AI, including **fairness constraints**, **bias auditing**, **continuous monitoring**, and **diverse development teams**. These strategies help ensure that AI systems operate in a fair, ethical, and transparent manner.

The chapter concluded with a **real-world example** of **discriminatory outcomes in AI-based loan approval systems**, illustrating the risks of bias in AI and the importance of addressing these issues through auditing, fairness constraints, and greater transparency.

As AI continues to be deployed across a wide range of sectors, addressing discrimination in AI systems will be crucial to ensure that these technologies benefit all people equally, without perpetuating existing inequalities.

CHAPTER 11

AI for Social Good

Using AI to Solve Global Challenges: AI Applications in Healthcare, Climate Change, and Poverty

Artificial intelligence has the potential to drive substantial positive change across the globe, addressing critical challenges like healthcare access, climate change, and poverty. AI's ability to process vast amounts of data, make predictions, and automate complex tasks makes it an invaluable tool in solving pressing global issues.

1. **AI in Healthcare**:
   o **Early Disease Detection**: AI is already being used in healthcare to detect diseases like cancer, diabetes, and cardiovascular conditions at early stages when they are more treatable. Machine learning algorithms can analyze medical images (e.g., X-rays, MRIs) or genetic data to identify patterns that may go unnoticed by human doctors.
   o **Personalized Medicine**: AI can help create personalized treatment plans by analyzing patient data and predicting how different treatments will affect an individual based on their genetic makeup and health history.
   o **Healthcare Access**: AI-driven telemedicine and diagnostic tools are

helping extend healthcare access to remote or underserved areas. AI can assist doctors in diagnosing conditions in locations with limited access to specialists, improving healthcare delivery in rural or low-income areas.

2. **AI in Climate Change**:
   o **Climate Modeling and Predictions**: AI can process vast amounts of environmental data to improve climate modeling and predict the effects of climate change. Machine learning models can simulate various climate scenarios, providing policymakers with the insights needed to mitigate the impact of climate change.
   o **Energy Efficiency**: AI systems are being used to optimize energy consumption in buildings, industries, and cities. Smart grids, powered by AI, can predict energy demand and adjust supply, reducing waste and promoting energy efficiency.
   o **Renewable Energy**: AI is also being used to optimize the production and distribution of renewable energy, such as wind and solar power. By predicting weather patterns and energy demand, AI can help maximize the efficiency of renewable energy sources, making them more reliable and cost-effective.

3. **AI in Poverty**:
   o **Financial Inclusion**: AI-driven financial technologies, like mobile banking and

microfinance platforms, are helping bring financial services to people in low-income or underserved communities. These services help individuals access loans, savings accounts, and other financial tools that were previously out of reach.

o **Job Creation and Workforce Development**: AI can help identify skills gaps in the workforce and recommend training programs to help people gain employment in emerging industries. Additionally, AI applications can assist in creating new job opportunities by automating certain tasks while also opening up more innovative roles.

o **Social Safety Nets**: AI can assist governments and NGOs in delivering social welfare programs more effectively by analyzing data to identify those most in need and ensuring resources are allocated efficiently.

AI's ability to tackle complex, multifaceted issues makes it a powerful tool for addressing some of the world's most urgent problems. However, it's important to ensure that AI is used ethically and responsibly to maximize its benefits for society as a whole.

Ethical AI for Good: Aligning AI with Humanitarian Goals

While AI holds tremendous potential for positive social impact, it is essential that its development and deployment align with **humanitarian goals**. Ethical AI for good requires that the benefits of AI are distributed equitably, and that AI systems are designed and implemented with fairness, transparency, and accountability in mind.

1. **Ensuring Fairness**: As AI is deployed to address global challenges, it must be designed to avoid reinforcing existing inequalities. Whether it's ensuring that AI in healthcare is equally effective for all demographic groups, or that AI-driven social welfare programs don't inadvertently leave certain communities behind, fairness is critical.

2. **Transparency and Accountability**: AI for social good should be transparent, meaning that stakeholders—whether it be governments, businesses, or individuals—understand how decisions are being made. AI systems must be explainable, especially in high-stakes areas like healthcare and disaster relief, where decisions can directly affect human lives.

3. **Alignment with Human Rights**: Ethical AI for good must be aligned with **human rights** principles. This means that AI systems must respect privacy, prevent discrimination, and promote individual freedom and dignity. AI should be used as a tool for enhancing human well-being, not diminishing it.

4. **Human-Centered Design**: AI systems should prioritize human welfare, ensuring that technological advancements do not come at the expense of human values. Human-centered

design places the needs, experiences, and rights of individuals at the core of AI development, helping ensure that the technology serves people in ways that are inclusive, equitable, and just.

Examples of Ethical AI for Good:

- **AI for Global Health**: AI is being used to monitor and track the spread of infectious diseases like COVID-19, helping governments and health organizations respond more effectively. Ethical AI in this context would involve ensuring that data privacy is respected, and that the data used is representative of all populations.
- **AI for Climate Justice**: AI systems used to combat climate change should prioritize the needs of vulnerable communities, such as those in low-income regions or small island nations, who are disproportionately affected by climate change.

Challenges and Opportunities: Balancing Profit with Social Impact

One of the main challenges in deploying AI for social good is the balance between **profit** and **social impact**. Many AI-driven solutions are developed by private companies, which are often motivated by profit. However, when AI is used to address global challenges like healthcare, poverty, and climate change, the social impact becomes just as important, if not more so, than the financial gain.

1. **The Profit Motive**: AI companies are driven by the potential for financial gain, and this can sometimes conflict with the goal of addressing global challenges. For example, companies might prioritize the development of AI technologies that are commercially viable, rather than those that address urgent humanitarian needs.

2. **Social Impact Goals**: Organizations working on AI for social good must ensure that their projects are focused on long-term social impact rather than short-term profits. This might mean that companies need to adopt business models that prioritize **social responsibility**, such as by reinvesting profits into community-focused AI initiatives or collaborating with nonprofit organizations and governments to tackle global issues.

3. **Cross-Sector Collaboration**: One way to balance profit with social impact is through collaboration between the private sector, public sector, and civil society. Governments and NGOs can provide funding, regulation, and expertise, while companies bring innovation, technological know-how, and efficiency. Such partnerships can help ensure that AI projects benefit society as a whole.

Opportunities in Balancing Profit with Social Impact:

- **Inclusive Business Models**: Companies can develop AI solutions that serve the underserved, such as AI-powered microfinance or telemedicine services that provide affordable access to financial services or healthcare.

- **Impact Investing**: Investors can play a role in supporting AI projects that prioritize social impact by providing funding to startups and organizations focused on solving global challenges, rather than those focused solely on profit.

Real-World Example: AI Applications in Disaster Response and Recovery

AI has already shown great promise in **disaster response and recovery**, where it can be used to save lives, reduce human suffering, and accelerate recovery efforts. AI systems can analyze vast amounts of data in real time, providing emergency responders with critical information to make faster, more accurate decisions.

1. **Disaster Prediction**:
    - o AI can help predict natural disasters such as hurricanes, earthquakes, or floods. Machine learning models can analyze weather patterns, seismic activity, and historical data to provide early warnings and improve preparedness.
    - o **Example**: AI-based systems are being used by meteorologists to predict hurricanes and their paths, allowing governments and organizations to evacuate vulnerable populations before disaster strikes.

2. **Disaster Response**:
   - o In the aftermath of a disaster, AI can help coordinate emergency response efforts by analyzing real-time data from social media, satellite images, and sensors. AI can help identify the most affected areas and prioritize resource distribution to ensure that aid reaches the people who need it most.
   - o **Example**: After the 2010 earthquake in Haiti, AI-based systems were used to analyze satellite images and assess the extent of damage, helping organizations like the Red Cross coordinate relief efforts more effectively.

3. **Recovery and Rebuilding**:
   - o AI can also assist in the recovery and rebuilding phase by optimizing resource allocation, monitoring infrastructure damage, and assessing rebuilding needs. AI systems can help prioritize reconstruction efforts based on the most urgent needs, ensuring that resources are used efficiently.
   - o **Example**: In the wake of wildfires in California, AI-driven drones have been used to assess damage to properties, identify areas where rebuilding is needed, and help track the recovery process.

Challenges in Disaster Response Using AI:

- **Data Privacy**: During disaster response efforts, sensitive personal data may be collected, such as location information or health records. Ensuring that this data is used responsibly and with consent is crucial.
- **Access and Inclusion**: AI applications for disaster response must be designed to ensure that they reach all affected communities, including marginalized or vulnerable groups, who may have limited access to technology.

Summary

In this chapter, we explored the potential of **AI for social good**, emphasizing its applications in addressing **global challenges** such as healthcare, climate change, and poverty. AI can be a powerful tool in improving healthcare access, mitigating the effects of climate change, and promoting financial inclusion. However, it is essential to ensure that AI is developed with **ethical principles** in mind, aligning technological advancements with humanitarian goals.

We also examined the **challenges and opportunities** in balancing **profit with social impact**, and the need for businesses, governments, and NGOs to collaborate to create AI solutions that benefit society as a whole. The chapter concluded with a **real-world example** of **AI applications in disaster response and recovery**, demonstrating how AI can save lives, improve recovery efforts, and optimize the allocation of resources in times of crisis.

As AI continues to evolve, its potential to drive social good is immense. However, it is crucial that we develop AI systems that are transparent, fair, and aligned with ethical standards to ensure that these technologies contribute positively to society, especially in solving the world's most pressing issues.

CHAPTER 12

Regulating AI: The Role of Government

The Need for AI Regulation: Why Governments Must Step In

As artificial intelligence continues to evolve and shape industries, governments around the world must consider how to regulate this powerful technology to ensure its safe, ethical, and equitable use. While AI has the potential to drive innovation and improve quality of life, it also brings about serious risks, including the potential for discrimination, privacy violations, economic disruption, and misuse in areas like surveillance or warfare.

Reasons for AI Regulation:

1. **Ensuring Safety and Security**: AI systems can have far-reaching effects, from autonomous vehicles on the road to AI algorithms used in healthcare. Without regulation, there is the risk that poorly designed or improperly tested AI systems could cause harm, either due to malfunctions or unintended consequences.
2. **Preventing Discrimination and Bias**: AI models are susceptible to biases, as they often learn from historical data that may contain racial, gender, or socioeconomic biases. Without government oversight, these biases can be perpetuated, leading to discriminatory outcomes

in areas such as hiring, loan approval, or law enforcement.

3. **Protecting Privacy and Rights**: AI often relies on vast amounts of personal data to function. Governments must step in to ensure that data privacy is respected, especially in the face of growing concerns over surveillance and data misuse. Regulations can help protect individuals' rights and ensure their data is handled responsibly.

4. **Promoting Accountability**: AI systems can make autonomous decisions, but accountability for these decisions remains a gray area. If an AI system causes harm, it may be unclear who should be held responsible—whether it's the developers, the company deploying the system, or the AI itself. Governments can help define accountability and ensure that there are clear mechanisms for addressing harm caused by AI systems.

5. **Encouraging Ethical AI Development**: By setting standards and guidelines for AI development, governments can promote the creation of AI technologies that align with ethical principles, including fairness, transparency, and respect for human rights.

AI regulation is not just a matter of mitigating risks—it's also about **ensuring that AI benefits all of society**, promoting innovation while safeguarding public interest and trust.

Current AI Regulations: Laws Governing AI, Such as the EU AI Act

Across the globe, governments are beginning to implement or consider various regulatory frameworks to manage the rapid rise of AI technologies. One of the most comprehensive and forward-thinking regulatory frameworks comes from the European Union (EU), which has taken a proactive approach to AI regulation. However, other regions, including the United States, China, and various international organizations, are also considering or implementing AI-related policies.

Key Examples of Current AI Regulations:

1. **EU AI Act**:
   - **Overview**: The **EU AI Act**, proposed in April 2021, is one of the first comprehensive legal frameworks for AI regulation in the world. It aims to regulate AI based on its risk to individuals and society, introducing **proportional regulation** that addresses higher-risk AI applications with stricter oversight, while allowing lower-risk applications to be regulated with more flexibility.
   - **Key Provisions**:
     - **Risk-Based Classification**: The EU AI Act classifies AI systems into four risk categories: **unacceptable risk, high risk, limited risk**, and **minimal risk**. High-risk AI systems (e.g., in

healthcare, law enforcement, or critical infrastructure) are subject to stricter regulatory requirements.

- **Requirements for High-Risk AI**: High-risk AI systems are required to meet specific standards for transparency, accountability, and documentation, including the obligation to perform rigorous testing and risk assessments before deployment.
- **Governance and Enforcement**: The Act proposes a centralized regulatory framework, with national authorities overseeing AI regulation and a European Artificial Intelligence Board coordinating efforts across member states.
- **Focus on Transparency and Explainability**: For high-risk AI systems, the EU AI Act emphasizes the need for transparency and explainability. Developers must ensure that their AI models are explainable to users, and individuals must be informed when they are interacting with AI systems.

2. **GDPR and AI**:
   - The **General Data Protection Regulation (GDPR)**, introduced by the EU in 2018, is another important piece of

legislation that impacts AI. The GDPR sets out strict guidelines for how personal data should be collected, stored, and processed, and it includes provisions related to AI and automated decision-making.

- **Key Provisions Relevant to AI**:
  - **Right to Explanation**: The GDPR grants individuals the **right to explanation** when they are subject to automated decision-making. This means that individuals can request an explanation when AI systems make decisions about them (e.g., in loan approvals, hiring, or credit scoring).
  - **Data Minimization**: The GDPR also requires AI systems to only use the minimum amount of personal data necessary for their function. This helps prevent over-collection and misuse of sensitive data.

3. **Other Global Initiatives**:
   - **China**: In 2021, China introduced a set of AI **ethics guidelines** that focus on ensuring AI serves national development goals while preventing risks related to privacy and security. China's government is also moving toward creating AI regulations that align with its broader tech policy agenda.

- o **United States**: While the U.S. has no overarching AI regulation at the federal level, several agencies, including the **Federal Trade Commission (FTC)** and the **National Institute of Standards and Technology (NIST)**, have published guidelines related to AI transparency, fairness, and accountability. The U.S. is currently focused on developing sector-specific AI regulations (e.g., in autonomous vehicles or healthcare).

Creating Fair and Effective AI Policies: Best Practices for Regulation

As AI continues to shape industries and societies, governments must adopt **fair and effective AI policies** that balance the promotion of innovation with the protection of public interest. Creating policies that support the responsible development and use of AI is essential for fostering trust in AI technologies and maximizing their benefits.

Best Practices for Effective AI Regulation:

1. **Risk-Based Approach**:
    - o Regulation should be proportional to the risk that an AI system poses to individuals and society. **High-risk AI systems**, such as those used in healthcare, criminal justice, or autonomous vehicles, should be subject to more stringent regulation, while **low-risk AI** (e.g., AI used in video

games or personal assistants) should have lighter oversight.

- o **Example**: The EU AI Act's risk-based classification is a prime example of this approach, ensuring that AI systems are regulated in a way that reflects their potential impact on society.

2. **Transparency and Explainability**:
   - o AI regulations should mandate transparency in AI models, ensuring that decisions made by AI systems are explainable and understandable to users. This is particularly important in areas where AI decisions directly affect people's lives (e.g., healthcare, hiring, or credit).
   - o **Example**: The requirement for explainability in the EU AI Act ensures that users and regulators can scrutinize AI systems and understand the rationale behind decisions.

3. **Ethical Guidelines and Human Rights**:
   - o AI regulation should prioritize human rights and ethical considerations, such as fairness, accountability, and non-discrimination. AI systems should be designed to avoid bias and ensure that their outcomes are equitable for all groups.
   - o **Example**: The **OECD AI Principles** emphasize that AI systems should be transparent, accountable, and aligned

with human rights, ensuring that AI is used for the benefit of all.

4. **Stakeholder Collaboration**:
   o Policymakers should collaborate with a wide range of stakeholders, including tech companies, civil society organizations, and academics, to create AI regulations that are informed by diverse perspectives and expertise.
   o **Example**: The EU's multi-stakeholder approach to developing the AI Act has involved consultation with experts from various fields to ensure that the regulation addresses both the technological potential and the ethical risks of AI.

5. **International Cooperation**:
   o AI regulation is a global issue that requires international cooperation. Governments and organizations should work together to develop common standards and guidelines that ensure AI technologies are used responsibly across borders.
   o **Example**: The **OECD** and **UNESCO** are working on establishing international frameworks for AI governance, focusing on shared ethical principles and guidelines for AI development.

6. **Ongoing Review and Adaptation**:
   o AI regulation should be flexible and adaptive, able to evolve as the technology itself evolves. Continuous monitoring and

updating of regulations are necessary to keep pace with rapid advancements in AI.

- o **Example**: The **EU AI Act** includes provisions for continuous assessment and updates to its regulations, ensuring that the framework can adapt to emerging challenges and technologies.

Real-World Example: The EU's Approach to AI Regulation

The **European Union** has taken a pioneering role in AI regulation with its **AI Act** and other related policies. The EU AI Act, introduced in 2021, is the world's first attempt to create a comprehensive regulatory framework for AI that addresses ethical, legal, and societal issues. The Act categorizes AI systems based on their risk to individuals and society, ensuring that higher-risk systems are subject to stricter oversight and accountability.

1. **Risk Classification**:
   - o The Act classifies AI systems into four categories: **unacceptable risk**, **high risk**, **limited risk**, and **minimal risk**. High-risk AI applications, such as those in healthcare, transportation, or law enforcement, are subject to stringent requirements, including transparency, documentation, and regular audits.
2. **Governance and Enforcement**:
   - o The EU AI Act proposes a governance framework where national authorities in

EU member states are responsible for enforcing AI regulations. The Act also creates a European Artificial Intelligence Board to coordinate efforts and provide guidance on AI regulation across the EU.

3. **Transparency and Accountability**:
   o The Act places a strong emphasis on **transparency**, requiring AI developers to provide detailed documentation of how their models work, how decisions are made, and how potential risks are mitigated. It also mandates that individuals have the right to challenge decisions made by AI systems, particularly in high-risk domains.

4. **Human Rights and Ethical Considerations**:
   o The EU AI Act aligns AI regulation with fundamental **human rights**, ensuring that AI systems respect privacy, fairness, and non-discrimination. The Act includes provisions to address AI-related risks, such as the potential for bias, invasion of privacy, and violations of civil liberties.

Summary

In this chapter, we discussed the role of government in **regulating AI** to ensure its ethical use and minimize risks. We explored why AI regulation is necessary, including the need to ensure safety, fairness, and accountability in AI systems. We also examined

current AI regulations, such as the **EU AI Act**, which provides a comprehensive framework for managing AI risks based on their potential impact on society.

We provided **best practices** for creating effective AI policies, emphasizing a **risk-based approach**, **transparency, ethics, stakeholder collaboration**, and **international cooperation**. The chapter concluded with a **real-world example** of the **EU's approach to AI regulation**, showcasing its efforts to balance innovation with responsible oversight.

As AI continues to evolve, government regulation will be key to ensuring that AI technologies are used for the benefit of society while minimizing their potential harms. Effective regulation will help build public trust in AI and ensure that its development aligns with ethical principles and human rights.

CHAPTER 13

AI and the Future of Work

AI's Impact on Employment: Automation, Job Displacement, and Job Creation

Artificial Intelligence is poised to significantly reshape the workforce, with both **opportunities and challenges** arising from its integration into industries across the globe. As AI technologies advance, the way work is performed will be transformed, leading to **automation, job displacement**, and **job creation**. The key to understanding AI's impact on employment lies in recognizing how these changes will unfold in various sectors.

1. **Automation and Job Displacement**:
   o **Automation**: AI and robotics have already begun automating routine and repetitive tasks, especially in sectors like manufacturing, logistics, and administrative work. Tasks that involve data processing, pattern recognition, or decision-making based on predefined rules are increasingly being handled by AI systems.
      ▪ **Example**: In manufacturing, robotic arms and automated assembly lines powered by AI are replacing manual labor in many industries. In offices, AI systems can now handle tasks such as

scheduling, data entry, and even basic customer service (e.g., chatbots).

- o **Job Displacement**: As AI systems take over these tasks, many jobs—especially those involving manual or repetitive work—are at risk of being displaced. For example, factory workers, clerical workers, and even some service workers may find their jobs at risk as AI-powered systems replace tasks they once performed.
- o **Example**: In the **retail industry**, self-checkout machines and automated inventory systems are replacing cashiers and stock clerks, potentially displacing thousands of jobs worldwide.

2. **Job Creation**:
   - o **New Roles**: While AI will undoubtedly lead to job displacement in certain sectors, it will also create new roles and opportunities in others. AI is expected to create jobs in areas such as AI development, data science, machine learning engineering, and robotics. These roles require specialized skills that will be in high demand as AI becomes more prevalent.
   - o **Emerging Sectors**: AI is also opening up entirely new sectors that didn't exist before. For example, the rise of AI-powered technologies has led to the creation of jobs in **AI ethics, AI**

regulation, **AI system maintenance**, and **human-AI collaboration** roles. Additionally, industries like **healthcare technology**, **autonomous vehicles**, and **sustainable energy** are likely to experience growth, providing new job opportunities.

- o **AI-Augmented Roles**: Rather than fully replacing human workers, AI is increasingly augmenting existing roles. This means that many jobs will evolve to require human-AI collaboration, where workers use AI tools to perform tasks more efficiently and creatively. For example, AI tools are being used by doctors to assist with diagnoses or by marketers to analyze consumer behavior and optimize advertising strategies.

3. **Balancing Job Displacement and Creation**:
   - o **Transitioning to New Roles**: As AI reshapes the workforce, it's crucial to strike a balance between the jobs that will be displaced and those that will be created. While AI may replace some roles, it can also empower individuals to take on more complex, creative, and decision-making tasks that were previously out of reach.
   - o **Economic Shifts**: The shift towards AI and automation will likely cause disruptions in labor markets. Governments, businesses, and educational institutions must work

together to ensure that workers are equipped with the necessary skills to transition to new roles, thus minimizing the negative impacts of automation.

Preparing the Workforce for AI: Education, Reskilling, and Upskilling

As AI continues to transform industries, **education**, **reskilling**, and **upskilling** are key to ensuring that the workforce can adapt to new demands. The future of work will require workers to embrace new technologies, develop a diverse set of skills, and stay up-to-date with the rapidly evolving landscape of AI.

1. **Education for the AI Age**:
   o **Early Education and STEM**: To ensure that the workforce is prepared for the future, early education systems should emphasize **STEM (Science, Technology, Engineering, and Mathematics)** education, as these fields will form the foundation of many AI-driven industries. AI literacy should be integrated into curricula at all levels, from primary schools to universities, so that students have the skills to understand, work with, and innovate with AI technologies.
   o **Encouraging Diversity in Tech**: AI development and research are often dominated by certain groups, particularly men and those from high-income countries. To prepare a more diverse and

inclusive workforce for AI, it is essential to encourage **underrepresented groups**—such as women, people of color, and those from lower-income backgrounds—to pursue careers in AI and technology. This will not only improve equity but also drive innovation by bringing diverse perspectives to the table.

2. **Reskilling and Upskilling the Current Workforce**:
   - **Reskilling**: Reskilling involves teaching workers new skills to help them transition into different jobs or industries. As automation replaces certain jobs, reskilling programs will be crucial for workers to remain employable in AI-driven sectors. For example, factory workers who have lost their jobs due to automation might be reskilled to work in AI-driven maintenance or data analysis roles.
   - **Upskilling**: Upskilling is the process of enhancing the skills of workers in their current jobs. This can involve learning to work alongside AI systems or learning new technologies that improve productivity and decision-making. For example, retail employees could be trained to use AI-powered customer service tools or logistics workers could learn to operate autonomous delivery drones.

- Corporate Training Programs: Many businesses are already investing in reskilling and upskilling their employees. Companies like **Amazon** and **Walmart** have developed internal programs to train workers in technical fields, such as robotics, data analysis, and cloud computing, to help them stay relevant as AI technologies are implemented in their industries.

3. **Public-Private Partnerships for Workforce Development**:
    - Governments and businesses must collaborate to develop policies and programs that support workforce transformation in the age of AI. Public-private partnerships can help create **training programs, certifications**, and **job placement initiatives** that equip workers with the necessary skills to thrive in AI-driven environments.
    - **Example**: In Singapore, the government has launched initiatives like the **SkillsFuture program**, which provides citizens with access to training programs in emerging technologies such as AI, data analytics, and digital marketing, ensuring that the workforce can adapt to changes brought about by automation and AI.

Ethical Considerations in Employment: Ensuring Fairness and Equality

As AI systems are increasingly used in employment-related processes such as hiring, promotions, and pay, it is essential to ensure that these systems do not perpetuate discrimination or inequality. **Ethical considerations** in employment revolve around ensuring that AI systems are **fair, transparent**, and **accountable**, and that they respect the rights of workers.

1. **Bias in AI Employment Systems**:
   o **Hiring Algorithms**: AI-powered recruitment tools and hiring algorithms are being used by many organizations to streamline candidate selection. However, these systems can inadvertently perpetuate existing biases. If the training data for these systems is biased (e.g., reflecting gender or racial disparities in past hiring decisions), the AI system will likely reinforce those biases, leading to discriminatory outcomes.
   o **Example**: In 2018, **Amazon** scrapped its AI recruitment tool after discovering that it was biased against female candidates. The tool had been trained on resumes submitted to Amazon over a ten-year period, which were predominantly male, leading to the algorithm favoring male applicants.
2. **Ensuring Fairness**:

- o **Fairness Constraints**: To ensure fairness in AI-based employment systems, fairness constraints should be implemented to avoid discrimination based on race, gender, age, or other irrelevant factors. AI systems must be regularly audited and adjusted to identify and address potential biases.
- o **Transparency in Hiring**: Employers must provide transparency in AI-based hiring processes. Applicants should be informed about how their data is being used and how decisions are being made, and they should have the opportunity to appeal or challenge decisions if they believe they have been unfairly treated.

3. **AI and Worker Rights**:
   - o As AI systems are integrated into workplaces, ensuring that **workers' rights** are protected becomes increasingly important. This includes ensuring that AI does not infringe on workers' privacy, that it does not replace human workers in ways that create unjust economic disparities, and that AI does not exacerbate existing inequalities.
   - o **Example**: In the gig economy, AI is increasingly being used to monitor workers, such as delivery drivers or ride-share drivers, to optimize their schedules and workloads. It's essential to ensure that workers' privacy is respected and that AI systems are not used to exploit them,

such as through unfair performance metrics or lack of worker benefits.

Real-World Example: Automation in Manufacturing and Its Effects on Workers

The **manufacturing industry** has been one of the most affected by automation, particularly in the form of AI-powered robots and machines that can perform tasks that were once carried out by human workers. While automation has led to greater efficiency and cost reduction for companies, it has also led to job displacement and economic disruption for workers in certain regions.

1. **Job Displacement**: In traditional manufacturing industries, AI and automation systems have replaced many low-skilled manual labor jobs. Robots can now perform tasks such as assembly, packaging, and quality control, reducing the need for human workers in these areas.
   - **Example**: In the automotive industry, **robots** have been widely adopted to assemble vehicles, perform welding, and handle dangerous tasks that were previously done by human workers. This has led to a reduction in factory jobs in many countries, particularly for lower-skilled workers.
2. **Job Creation and Transformation**: While automation has displaced some jobs, it has also created new roles in areas such as **robot maintenance**, **AI system development**, and

data analysis. Additionally, as manufacturing becomes more automated, the demand for workers who can design, manage, and troubleshoot automated systems is increasing.

- o **Example**: In the automotive industry, roles like **robotics engineers** and **AI specialists** are in higher demand as companies look to develop, maintain, and optimize their automated systems.

3. **Balancing the Effects**: Many manufacturing companies have implemented reskilling programs to help displaced workers transition to new roles in more technology-driven areas. For example, some companies are providing training for workers to become proficient in **AI system management** and **robotic maintenance**, ensuring that workers can adapt to the changing landscape.

Summary

In this chapter, we explored the impact of **AI on employment**, covering both the **positive and negative consequences** of automation. We discussed the challenges of **job displacement**, the creation of new **AI-driven roles**, and the importance of **reskilling and upskilling** to prepare the workforce for an AI-powered future.

We also examined **ethical considerations** in employment, including the need to ensure **fairness** and

transparency in AI-based employment systems to prevent discrimination. The chapter concluded with a **real-world example** of **automation in manufacturing**, illustrating the effects of AI on workers and highlighting the importance of balancing technological advancement with worker rights and opportunities for reskilling.

As AI continues to transform the workforce, it is crucial for businesses, governments, and educational institutions to work together to ensure that workers are equipped with the skills they need to thrive in the future of work, while also ensuring that AI is used ethically and responsibly.

CHAPTER 14

Designing for Safety in AI Systems

AI Safety: Ensuring AI Systems Are Safe to Use

As AI systems become more pervasive in society, from healthcare to transportation to finance, ensuring that these systems are **safe** to use is of utmost importance. AI systems, especially those that operate autonomously or interact directly with human users, must be designed and implemented in ways that prevent harm, minimize risk, and ensure they behave as intended in various conditions.

Key Aspects of AI Safety:

1. **Preventing Harm**: One of the primary concerns in AI safety is ensuring that the system does not cause physical, financial, or psychological harm to individuals. Whether it's an autonomous vehicle, a medical diagnostic tool, or an AI-powered hiring system, the potential for harm must be thoroughly considered and mitigated during design.
2. **Ensuring Ethical Behavior**: Safe AI systems should adhere to ethical guidelines, such as fairness, accountability, and transparency. This includes avoiding harmful biases, making decisions that respect human rights, and ensuring that the system's behavior aligns with societal values.

3. **Reliability and Predictability**: AI systems should be reliable and predictable, especially in high-risk environments like healthcare or autonomous driving. An AI system should act consistently and as expected under varying conditions, ensuring that users can trust its decisions and actions.

4. **Redundancy and Fail-Safes**: Just as with critical infrastructure systems, AI systems, especially those used in high-risk applications, should have built-in redundancy and fail-safe mechanisms. These mechanisms can help the system safely recover from failures and continue to function in an expected, secure manner.

5. **Accountability**: In case of failure or harm, it must be clear who is responsible for the design, implementation, and operation of the AI system. Clear accountability structures ensure that developers, organizations, and regulators take responsibility for the actions of AI systems.

Creating Robust AI Systems: Preventing AI Failures and Ensuring Reliability

For AI systems to be considered **safe**, they must be both **robust** and **reliable**. Robustness refers to the AI's ability to handle unexpected or adverse conditions without failing or behaving erratically, while reliability means that the AI consistently performs as intended under normal and stressful circumstances.

1. **Handling Edge Cases**:

- o **Edge cases** refer to situations that fall outside the typical conditions the system is trained on. Robust AI systems should be capable of identifying and handling edge cases appropriately. For example, an autonomous vehicle may need to respond to situations that its training data didn't cover, such as a sudden, unexpected road hazard or an unusual weather condition.
- o **Approach**: Developers should test AI systems under a variety of edge cases, simulating as many rare but critical scenarios as possible. This includes stress testing AI models in environments that are unpredictable or have incomplete data.

2. **Continuous Learning and Adaptability**:
   - o **Self-Correction**: Robust AI systems can adapt to new information and situations over time. In some systems, especially those involving machine learning, continual learning may be necessary to adapt to new data and evolving environments. However, this must be done carefully to avoid unpredictable behaviors.
   - o **Approach**: Developers must ensure that AI systems can safely update or retrain themselves to handle new conditions, without losing control or introducing errors into the system.

3. **Model Generalization**:

- o AI systems must generalize well to real-world scenarios. Generalization is the ability of an AI model to make accurate predictions or decisions on new, unseen data based on its training. Overfitting—where a model is too specifically tailored to the training data—can make the system unreliable when faced with real-world situations.
- o **Approach**: To prevent overfitting, developers should use diverse, representative datasets, and employ techniques such as cross-validation and regularization to ensure the AI model performs well across a range of scenarios.

4. **Error Detection and Recovery**:
   - o **Error Detection**: AI systems should have built-in mechanisms for detecting when they are not functioning correctly. This could be through self-monitoring or monitoring by human operators.
   - o **Recovery**: When an error is detected, the system should be able to recover gracefully, either by switching to a fail-safe mode or by alerting human operators to intervene if necessary.
   - o **Approach**: AI systems should have automated diagnostic tools and error-correction algorithms to minimize downtime and maintain high reliability.

Testing and Verification: Strategies for Safe AI Deployment

Thorough testing and verification are essential to ensure the safety of AI systems before they are deployed. Rigorous testing is needed to ensure that the AI behaves as expected and adheres to all safety and ethical standards.

1. **Simulation and Testing in Virtual Environments**:
   o AI systems, particularly those that involve autonomous decision-making (like self-driving cars or drones), can be tested in **virtual environments** or **simulations** before being deployed in the real world. These simulations provide a controlled setting in which the system's behavior can be closely monitored and refined without the risk of causing harm.
   o **Example**: Autonomous vehicle companies like **Waymo** and **Tesla** use large-scale simulations to test their AI systems' responses to different driving scenarios, weather conditions, and emergency situations.
2. **Real-World Testing with Monitoring**:
   o Even after extensive simulation testing, AI systems must be tested in real-world environments to ensure their reliability and robustness under natural conditions. These tests should be done incrementally, starting with small-scale pilots and

expanding as the system proves its safety and effectiveness.

- o **Approach**: In real-world testing, **continuous monitoring** is crucial. Developers and operators should monitor the system's performance closely during early stages of deployment, with mechanisms in place to intervene in case of any safety concerns.

3. **Human Oversight and Control**:
   - o Testing AI systems should involve **human oversight**, especially in high-risk areas like healthcare, finance, and autonomous driving. Human operators should be able to intervene in case the AI system makes a decision that could cause harm or deviate from its intended behavior.
   - o **Example**: In autonomous vehicles, although the vehicle may be capable of driving itself, human drivers are still required to supervise the vehicle and take control in case of malfunction or unexpected events.

4. **Independent Auditing and Validation**:
   - o **Independent Auditing**: AI systems, especially those used in critical sectors, should undergo **independent audits** to ensure their safety and compliance with legal and ethical standards. Third-party experts can assess the AI's performance, fairness, transparency, and robustness,

providing a fresh perspective on potential risks.

- o **Validation**: Validation involves checking that an AI system meets its specifications and performs the required tasks without unintended behaviors. This is especially important in high-risk applications like medical devices, where incorrect decisions can have life-altering consequences.

Real-World Example: Ensuring Safety in Autonomous Vehicles

One of the most challenging areas for AI safety is in the development of **autonomous vehicles (AVs)**. These vehicles rely on AI to make decisions in real-time about how to navigate roads, avoid obstacles, and interact with other drivers, pedestrians, and road conditions. The stakes are high, as a failure in an autonomous vehicle system can result in loss of life, injury, or property damage.

1. **Safety Standards**:
   - o The **SAE (Society of Automotive Engineers)** has defined a set of levels for driving automation, ranging from **Level 0** (no automation) to **Level 5** (full automation). At higher levels of autonomy, AVs must ensure that their AI systems are capable of handling a vast range of scenarios, including **edge cases** (rare but critical events) that human

drivers could manage but which the AI might struggle with.

o Safety standards like the **ISO 26262** standard for functional safety in automotive systems provide guidance on how to ensure that safety-critical systems, including those used in AVs, are designed, implemented, and tested to prevent failures.

2. **Testing AVs for Safety**:

o **Simulation Testing**: Companies like **Waymo** and **Uber** have invested heavily in simulation testing, where AV systems can be subjected to a wide range of driving scenarios that are difficult to recreate in the real world. These include complex driving conditions, adverse weather, and emergency scenarios.

o **Real-World Testing**: Even with extensive simulation testing, AVs must undergo **real-world testing** to ensure they perform safely under normal driving conditions. This involves gradual deployment on public roads under controlled conditions, with human drivers in the vehicle who can take over if needed.

o **Example**: In 2018, an Uber self-driving car was involved in a fatal accident with a pedestrian. The vehicle's AI system failed to recognize the pedestrian in time, and the backup human driver did not intervene quickly enough. This tragic incident underscored the importance of thorough testing, monitoring, and human oversight in ensuring the safety of AV systems.

3. **Redundancy and Fail-Safes**:
   - Autonomous vehicles are designed with multiple levels of redundancy to ensure they can still function safely in case of system failures. For example, AVs often have backup sensors, cameras, and algorithms that can take over if the primary system fails. They also include emergency braking systems that can be activated automatically in case of an impending collision.

Summary

In this chapter, we explored the importance of **safety** in AI system design, particularly in **high-risk applications** like autonomous vehicles. We discussed how to ensure that AI systems are **robust** and **reliable** through proper testing, verification, and continuous monitoring. Key strategies for ensuring safe deployment include **simulation testing**, **real-world testing**, **human oversight**, and **independent audits**.

We also highlighted a **real-world example** of **ensuring safety in autonomous vehicles**, focusing on the challenges of developing AI systems that can safely navigate complex, unpredictable environments. The tragic incident involving an Uber autonomous vehicle serves as a reminder of the need for thorough testing, fail-safes, and human-in-the-loop systems to prevent AI failures and ensure public safety.

As AI systems continue to evolve and become more integrated into everyday life, ensuring their safety will be paramount in building public trust, preventing harm, and ensuring that these technologies benefit society as a whole.

CHAPTER 15

Sustainability in AI

Environmental Impact of AI: Energy Consumption, Carbon Footprint of Training Models

As artificial intelligence continues to advance, its **environmental impact** has become a growing concern, particularly in terms of **energy consumption** and **carbon footprint**. AI models, especially those used in machine learning and deep learning, require significant computational resources for both training and inference. These operations, especially when done at scale, can lead to substantial environmental costs.

1. **Energy Consumption**:
   o **Training AI Models**: Training large AI models, especially deep learning models, requires enormous computational power. The process of training a neural network involves processing vast amounts of data, often across thousands of machines, for extended periods. The energy consumed by these operations is considerable, especially for state-of-the-art models in fields like natural language processing (NLP), computer vision, and autonomous driving.
   o **Example**: The training of large language models like OpenAI's **GPT-3** and Google's **BERT** involves running computations on clusters of high-

performance GPUs and TPUs (tensor processing units) over weeks or months, leading to high energy usage.

2. **Carbon Footprint**:
   - o The carbon footprint of AI is directly linked to the energy sources used by the data centers hosting the AI models. If the data centers rely on non-renewable energy sources, such as coal or natural gas, the carbon emissions can be significant. The environmental impact of AI is amplified when the data center's energy usage grows in tandem with the scale of AI deployments.
   - o **Example**: Research has shown that training a large AI model can emit as much carbon dioxide as the lifetime emissions of several cars. This highlights the urgent need for more sustainable practices in AI development.

3. **Impact of Data Centers**:
   - o **Data Centers** are the backbone of AI, as they house the servers that store data and run AI algorithms. Data centers are responsible for a substantial portion of global energy consumption. The scale of AI applications in industries such as cloud computing, online services, and research has only increased the demand for energy-intensive data centers.
   - o **Global Energy Consumption**: According to a report from the **International Energy Agency (IEA)**,

data centers account for around 1-2% of global electricity demand. As AI systems become more pervasive, this number is expected to rise unless significant strides are made toward energy-efficient practices.

Designing Green AI Systems: Optimizing AI for Energy Efficiency

Given the growing environmental concerns surrounding AI, there is an increasing push for **green AI**—AI systems that are **designed for energy efficiency** and **sustainability**. The focus is on minimizing the carbon footprint and energy consumption of AI systems while maintaining their performance.

1. **Efficient Algorithms**:
    - **Model Optimization**: One of the most effective ways to make AI systems more energy-efficient is by optimizing the algorithms themselves. This involves reducing the complexity of AI models without sacrificing performance. Smaller models that are more efficient in terms of computation require less energy for both training and inference.
    - **Pruning**: **Pruning** involves removing unnecessary parameters or weights from a neural network to reduce its size and complexity. This not only improves the model's efficiency but also reduces the

amount of computational power needed to run the model.

- o **Quantization**: **Quantization** is the process of reducing the precision of the numbers used to represent data in neural networks. This reduces the memory and computational requirements of models, making them more energy-efficient.

2. **Hardware Improvements**:
   - o **Specialized Hardware**: Advances in hardware, such as **energy-efficient processors, TPUs**, and **ASICs (Application-Specific Integrated Circuits)**, can significantly improve the energy efficiency of AI systems. These processors are optimized for specific AI tasks and can perform them more efficiently than general-purpose CPUs or GPUs.
   - o **Hardware Accelerators**: AI hardware accelerators like **FPGAs (Field-Programmable Gate Arrays)** and **ASICs** are increasingly being used in data centers to speed up AI computations and reduce energy consumption. These specialized hardware components are designed to handle AI-specific workloads more efficiently, reducing the energy footprint of AI systems.

3. **Energy-Efficient Data Centers**:
   - o **Renewable Energy**: One of the most effective ways to reduce the environmental impact of AI is by

transitioning data centers to use **renewable energy** sources such as solar, wind, or hydroelectric power. Many major tech companies are already making significant strides in this area.

- o **Cooling Techniques**: Data centers require significant cooling to prevent overheating of servers. Innovative cooling techniques, such as **liquid cooling** and **using ambient temperatures in colder climates**, are being adopted to reduce energy usage.
- o **Edge Computing: Edge computing** involves processing data closer to where it is generated (e.g., on devices or local servers) rather than sending it to a central data center. By reducing the need for long-distance data transmission and processing, edge computing can reduce both energy consumption and latency.

The Future of Sustainable AI: Balancing Technological Progress with Environmental Concerns

As AI technology advances, balancing **technological progress** with **environmental sustainability** will be a key challenge. While AI has the potential to help tackle pressing global challenges like climate change and resource management, it also has the potential to exacerbate environmental problems if not designed and deployed responsibly.

1. **AI for Environmental Sustainability**:

- o **Climate Change Mitigation**: AI can be used to tackle climate change by improving energy efficiency, optimizing renewable energy grids, and predicting and modeling climate patterns. AI-driven solutions can help monitor emissions, reduce waste, and enable smarter management of natural resources.
- o **AI for Circular Economy**: AI is also being applied in the **circular economy** to optimize the use of resources and reduce waste. AI-powered systems can improve recycling processes, help design products that are easier to recycle, and track the lifecycle of materials used in manufacturing.

2. **Green AI as a Long-Term Goal**:
   - o **Sustainable Innovation**: As AI technologies continue to evolve, the focus on **sustainability** should become a fundamental aspect of innovation. This means incorporating **energy efficiency** and **sustainable practices** into AI research and development from the outset, ensuring that the long-term benefits of AI outweigh its environmental costs.
   - o **AI and Carbon Neutrality**: Many companies, including **Google**, **Microsoft**, and **Amazon**, are working towards **carbon neutrality** by offsetting their emissions through investments in renewable energy and carbon credits.

Incorporating green AI practices into these companies' AI systems is a crucial step toward achieving these goals.

3. **Collaboration for Sustainable AI**:
   o Governments, tech companies, and environmental organizations must work together to create regulations and incentives that promote the development of **green AI**. This collaboration can drive innovation in AI technologies that are both **powerful and environmentally responsible**.
   o **Policy Support**: Governments can encourage sustainability in AI by providing grants, subsidies, and tax incentives to companies that develop energy-efficient AI technologies or use renewable energy sources in their operations. International cooperation is also critical in setting global standards for AI sustainability.

Real-World Example: Google's Efforts to Make AI Data Centers More Energy-Efficient

Google is one of the leaders in making AI and data center operations more energy-efficient. As part of its commitment to sustainability, Google has implemented several initiatives aimed at reducing the energy consumption and carbon footprint of its AI-driven services.

1. **Renewable Energy**:

- **100% Renewable Energy**: In 2017, Google became the first major company to match its entire **annual energy consumption** with **renewable energy** purchases. This includes the energy required to run its data centers, which are integral to its AI operations.
- **Long-Term Sustainability Goals**: Google continues to invest in renewable energy projects, such as solar and wind farms, to ensure that its AI-powered services run on clean energy.

2. **Energy-Efficient Data Centers**:
   - **AI for Energy Efficiency**: Google uses AI itself to optimize the energy efficiency of its data centers. The company's **DeepMind AI** system has been used to predict and manage energy consumption in its data centers, improving efficiency by adjusting cooling and heating systems in real-time. This has resulted in a **40% reduction in energy used for cooling**.
   - **Machine Learning for Cooling**: The DeepMind AI uses machine learning to predict the optimal temperature for servers and cooling systems, reducing the need for constant cooling and, thus, saving energy.

3. **Sustainable Hardware**:
   - Google has also worked on making its data center hardware more energy-efficient. By designing custom **TPUs (Tensor Processing Units)** for AI

workloads, Google has created specialized hardware that is optimized for energy efficiency, reducing the overall power consumption of its AI systems.

Google's efforts in sustainable AI and energy-efficient data centers serve as a model for other companies looking to reduce their carbon footprint while leveraging AI technologies. The company's approach underscores the importance of integrating sustainability into AI development and operations, ensuring that AI's potential for innovation does not come at the expense of the planet.

Summary

In this chapter, we explored the **environmental impact** of AI, focusing on the **energy consumption** and **carbon footprint** associated with training and deploying AI models. We discussed the need for **green AI** and explored strategies for designing **energy-efficient AI systems**, including optimizing algorithms, improving hardware, and using renewable energy sources.

We also examined the **future of sustainable AI**, emphasizing the need to balance **technological progress** with environmental concerns. AI can play a critical role in addressing global challenges like climate change, but it is essential that AI systems are developed with sustainability in mind.

The chapter concluded with a **real-world example** of **Google's efforts** to make AI data centers more energy-efficient, demonstrating how leading tech companies are leveraging AI to reduce energy consumption and carbon emissions.

As AI continues to evolve, it is crucial that the development of this transformative technology goes hand-in-hand with environmental responsibility. By prioritizing sustainability in AI, we can ensure that these powerful tools are used to enhance human life while minimizing their impact on the planet.

CHAPTER 16

The Ethics of AI in Surveillance

AI in Surveillance Systems: From Facial Recognition to Predictive Policing

Artificial intelligence has increasingly become a core component of **surveillance systems**, revolutionizing how governments, businesses, and organizations monitor individuals and groups. AI-powered surveillance technologies are now widely used for a variety of purposes, ranging from **public safety** to **crime prevention** to **social control**.

1. **Facial Recognition**:
   o One of the most well-known AI-powered surveillance technologies is **facial recognition**. This system uses AI to analyze and identify individuals based on unique facial features. It is commonly employed in public spaces like airports, train stations, and city streets, as well as in private spaces like retail stores and workplaces.
   o **Applications**: Facial recognition technology is used for security purposes, such as identifying suspects in criminal investigations, controlling access to secure areas, and verifying identities for payments or logins.
   o **Concerns**: While facial recognition can enhance security, it raises significant

ethical concerns, particularly regarding privacy and the potential for **mass surveillance**. When used without clear consent, facial recognition can lead to the tracking and profiling of individuals without their knowledge, raising questions about surveillance overreach.

2. **Predictive Policing**:
   o **Predictive policing** is another AI-driven surveillance tool that uses historical crime data and machine learning algorithms to predict where crimes are likely to occur or which individuals may commit crimes. Police departments in several cities around the world have adopted predictive policing technologies in an attempt to prevent crime before it happens.
   o **Applications**: Predictive policing systems are used to deploy law enforcement resources more effectively, identify crime hotspots, and predict the likelihood of repeat offenders. These systems typically rely on data from historical crime reports, geographic data, and other behavioral indicators.
   o **Concerns**: Predictive policing systems can reinforce existing biases in law enforcement. If the data used to train these systems reflects biases in the criminal justice system (e.g., over-policing in minority communities), AI systems may perpetuate these biases,

disproportionately targeting marginalized groups.

3. **Surveillance in Public Spaces**:
   o AI technologies are increasingly being integrated into surveillance cameras and drones used to monitor public spaces. This includes monitoring traffic, detecting suspicious activities, and tracking the movements of individuals in crowded areas.
   o **Applications**: AI-driven surveillance systems can analyze footage in real time, detecting anomalies or behaviors that may indicate criminal activity, such as loitering, crowd gatherings, or unattended bags in public spaces.
   o **Concerns**: The use of surveillance technologies in public spaces raises concerns about **freedom of movement** and **privacy**. The constant monitoring of individuals can create a chilling effect on personal freedoms, as people may feel that they are always being watched.

Ethical Concerns: Privacy, Freedom, and Autonomy in a Surveillance State

While AI-powered surveillance systems offer benefits such as enhanced security and crime prevention, they also raise significant **ethical concerns** related to **privacy**, **freedom**, and **autonomy**. The widespread deployment of these technologies, especially when not properly regulated, can lead to the creation of a

surveillance state, where individuals are constantly monitored, tracked, and analyzed without their knowledge or consent.

1. **Privacy**:
   - **Invasion of Privacy**: One of the most pressing ethical concerns surrounding AI-driven surveillance is the invasion of privacy. Surveillance technologies like facial recognition and predictive policing systems often collect and analyze personal data without individuals' explicit consent. This can lead to an erosion of personal privacy, as people may feel that they are being constantly monitored.
   - **Data Collection**: AI surveillance systems typically rely on the collection of large amounts of personal data, such as facial images, movements, and even behavioral patterns. Without proper safeguards, this data can be misused, either by being shared without consent or by falling into the wrong hands.
2. **Freedom and Autonomy**:
   - **Chilling Effect**: The presence of AI-driven surveillance systems in public spaces can create a **chilling effect** on personal freedoms. When people are aware that they are being monitored, they may alter their behavior, curtailing their freedom of speech, movement, or association. This is particularly

concerning in societies where political dissent or activism is discouraged.

- o **Loss of Autonomy**: In a surveillance state, the constant monitoring of individuals can lead to a loss of autonomy. When individuals know they are always being watched, they may feel compelled to conform to social norms or authority expectations, stifling creativity, independence, and personal expression.

3. **Discrimination and Bias**:
   - o AI surveillance systems can perpetuate existing societal inequalities, particularly when they are built on biased data. Predictive policing systems, for example, may disproportionately target certain racial or ethnic groups if they are trained on biased crime data. Similarly, facial recognition systems may have lower accuracy rates for people of color or women, leading to wrongful identifications and discriminatory outcomes.
   - o **Example**: In the United States, studies have shown that facial recognition systems tend to have higher error rates for Black people and women, leading to concerns about racial and gender-based discrimination in AI surveillance systems.

Designing Ethical Surveillance Systems: Ensuring Transparency and Fairness

To address the ethical concerns surrounding AI surveillance, it is crucial to design systems that prioritize **transparency**, **fairness**, and **accountability**. Ethical AI surveillance should respect individuals' privacy and autonomy while ensuring that the systems are used responsibly and fairly.

1. **Transparency**:
   o **Clear Disclosure**: People should be informed when they are being monitored by AI surveillance systems. Governments and businesses using AI for surveillance must be transparent about their data collection practices, how the data will be used, and the potential risks involved. Public awareness campaigns can help individuals understand the implications of these systems and make informed decisions.
   o **Accountability**: AI surveillance systems should be held accountable for their actions. This includes ensuring that the data collected is used for its intended purpose and that there are mechanisms in place to address potential misuse. Independent oversight bodies should be established to monitor the use of surveillance technologies and enforce compliance with ethical standards.
2. **Fairness**:

- ○ **Bias Mitigation**: AI surveillance systems should be designed to avoid discrimination and bias. This can be achieved by using diverse datasets to train AI models, regularly auditing these systems for fairness, and ensuring that the algorithms do not disproportionately affect specific groups.
- ○ **Inclusive Design**: Developers should ensure that AI surveillance systems are inclusive and do not target or marginalize specific groups. For example, facial recognition systems should be trained on diverse data that includes different racial, ethnic, and gender groups to ensure that the technology works fairly for everyone.

3. **Privacy Protections**:
   - ○ **Data Minimization**: AI surveillance systems should adhere to the principle of **data minimization**, which means that they should collect only the data necessary for their function and avoid collecting sensitive personal information unless absolutely required.
   - ○ **Anonymization**: When possible, data should be anonymized to protect individuals' identities. This can help ensure that personal information is not misused or exposed to unauthorized parties.

4. **Human Oversight**:
   - ○ **Human-in-the-Loop**: AI surveillance systems should include mechanisms for

human oversight, especially in cases where decisions may have significant consequences for individuals' rights or freedoms. For example, a human operator should be able to intervene if a facial recognition system incorrectly identifies a person or if predictive policing algorithms lead to unjust outcomes.

Real-World Example: China's Use of AI in Social Credit Systems

China's Social Credit System is one of the most well-known and controversial examples of AI-driven surveillance and social control. The system uses a combination of AI technologies, including facial recognition, to monitor citizens' behavior and assign them a **social credit score**. This score reflects an individual's behavior and actions, including their financial reliability, adherence to laws, and even personal social conduct.

1. **AI in the Social Credit System**:
    o **Surveillance**: China's social credit system relies on widespread surveillance of citizens, including AI-powered **facial recognition** systems in public places, tracking individuals' movements, purchases, and online activities. Data from these sources is used to generate a score that can influence a person's access to various services, including travel, loans, and housing.

o **Social Control**: A person's social credit score can be affected by actions deemed undesirable by the state, such as speaking out against the government, being involved in corrupt practices, or even associating with people who have low scores. Conversely, individuals who comply with state expectations and laws may receive rewards in the form of better opportunities, discounts, or privileges.

2. **Ethical Concerns**:
   o **Privacy Violations**: The social credit system has raised concerns about **privacy violations** and **mass surveillance**. The continuous monitoring of individuals, without their explicit consent, infringes on their right to privacy and autonomy.
   o **Social Control and Freedom**: The social credit system has been criticized for its potential to stifle personal freedoms. People may feel pressured to conform to state-approved behaviors and attitudes, leading to a loss of individual autonomy and freedom of expression.
   o **Discrimination**: There are also concerns about **discrimination** in the social credit system. Citizens who fall into certain demographic groups or who live in specific areas may be unfairly penalized, further exacerbating social inequalities.

3. **International Criticism**:
   o China's social credit system has faced widespread international criticism for its

authoritarian nature and its potential to create a surveillance state. Human rights organizations have raised alarms about the system's ability to suppress dissent, discriminate against vulnerable groups, and limit personal freedoms.

Summary

In this chapter, we examined the ethical implications of **AI in surveillance**, focusing on technologies like **facial recognition** and **predictive policing**, and the **privacy**, **freedom**, and **autonomy** concerns they raise. We discussed how AI-powered surveillance systems can lead to the creation of a **surveillance state** that erodes individual privacy and personal freedoms, while potentially reinforcing discrimination and bias.

We also explored **designing ethical surveillance systems** by focusing on **transparency, fairness, privacy protections**, and **human oversight**. Ensuring that AI surveillance systems are transparent, accountable, and non-discriminatory is essential to mitigating the ethical risks associated with these technologies.

The chapter concluded with a **real-world example** of **China's social credit system**, highlighting the ethical challenges posed by AI-driven surveillance and social control. This example serves as a cautionary tale of how AI can be used for social monitoring, creating serious concerns about human rights, privacy, and the potential for state overreach.

As AI surveillance technologies continue to develop, it is crucial for governments, businesses, and technologists to create safeguards that balance the benefits of security and efficiency with the need to protect individual rights and freedoms.

CHAPTER 17

Ethical Challenges in AI Development

The Role of Developers in AI Ethics: Creating Responsible AI Solutions

AI developers play a crucial role in ensuring that AI technologies are designed, deployed, and maintained responsibly. As the creators of AI systems, developers must take on the responsibility of embedding **ethical principles** into the development process to ensure that the resulting AI solutions are beneficial, fair, and aligned with societal values. This responsibility goes beyond technical proficiency and includes an understanding of the broader social and ethical implications of AI.

1. **Designing Ethical AI Systems**:
   o **Incorporating Ethics from the Start**: Ethical considerations should be integrated into AI development at every stage—from design and training to deployment and maintenance. Developers must consider the potential impact of their AI systems on individuals, communities, and society at large. For example, when designing an AI model, developers should ensure that the training data is diverse and representative to avoid biases in the system's predictions and decisions.
   o **Prioritizing Transparency**: Developers should strive for transparency in how

their AI systems work, especially when these systems impact people's lives in significant ways, such as in hiring, lending, or healthcare. This includes creating models that can be explained in clear, understandable terms and allowing users to understand how decisions are being made.

- **Engagement with Stakeholders**: Developers should also engage with a diverse range of stakeholders—including ethicists, social scientists, policymakers, and the affected communities—to ensure that their AI solutions reflect a broad spectrum of perspectives and address potential concerns early in the development process.

2. **Mitigating Harm**:
- Developers must ensure that AI systems are designed to **minimize harm**. This includes avoiding potential negative outcomes such as **discrimination, privacy violations**, and the **reinforcement of social inequalities**. Ethical AI design goes beyond preventing immediate harm and includes foreseeing long-term implications, such as economic displacement or societal divide due to automation.
- **Example**: When developing predictive policing systems, developers should actively address the risk that the AI model could reinforce existing racial or

socioeconomic biases present in historical data.

3. **Building Ethical AI by Design**:
   o Developers must adopt principles such as **fairness**, **accountability**, **privacy**, and **inclusivity** as core elements of their development process. They should consider these principles as essential, rather than optional, components of their AI systems.

Ethical Decision-Making in AI Development: Balancing Technical, Ethical, and Business Considerations

AI development often involves navigating a complex landscape where technical requirements, ethical considerations, and business objectives must be balanced. While the primary goal of developers is to create efficient and functional AI solutions, they must also consider the ethical implications of their decisions, ensuring that the solutions are aligned with public interest and human rights.

1. **Balancing Efficiency and Ethical Impact**:
   o **Technical Constraints**: Developers often face trade-offs between optimizing AI models for **accuracy** and ensuring they are **ethically sound**. For instance, making a model more accurate may require using large datasets that are biased or invasive of personal privacy. Developers must balance these trade-offs, considering both the technical

performance of the system and its broader societal impact.

- o **Business Pressures**: Companies developing AI may be under pressure to release products quickly and efficiently to stay competitive in the market. This creates a conflict between rapid deployment and ensuring that the AI system adheres to ethical standards. Ethical decision-making in AI requires developers to resist cutting corners in favor of business goals that could compromise the fairness, transparency, or privacy of the system.

2. **Incorporating Ethical Guidelines into Development Processes**:
   - o Ethical decision-making frameworks can guide developers in evaluating potential consequences, both positive and negative, of AI systems. Tools like **impact assessments**, **ethical audits**, and **bias detection** can help identify potential ethical dilemmas and guide developers toward solutions that prioritize fairness, justice, and societal well-being.
   - o **Example**: A developer working on a recommendation system for a social media platform might face a dilemma between optimizing the system to maximize engagement (and profit) and preventing the spread of misinformation or harmful content. Balancing these competing interests requires ethical

foresight and consideration of the broader societal consequences.

3. **The Role of Ethics in AI Governance**:
   o AI governance is an essential part of the development process, where ethical principles are incorporated into decision-making at higher organizational and regulatory levels. Developers should not only consider ethical implications during the design and development phase but should also engage in discussions around AI regulation, policy, and the wider societal implications of AI deployment.

The Responsibility of AI Researchers: Ethical Considerations in AI Research

AI researchers hold significant responsibility in ensuring that their work adheres to ethical standards. Research in AI often lays the foundation for the technologies that will be used in the real world, and the ethical choices made during the research phase can have lasting impacts on society.

1. **Ethical Research Practices**:
   o **Informed Consent**: When conducting AI research that involves personal data, researchers must ensure that participants provide **informed consent** and understand how their data will be used. AI researchers must also adhere to data protection laws and principles, such as

those outlined in the **General Data Protection Regulation (GDPR)**.

- o **Minimizing Bias in Data**: Researchers must take responsibility for ensuring that the data used in AI research is not biased. This includes choosing diverse and representative datasets that accurately reflect the populations the AI will serve, and rigorously testing models for potential biases.
- o **Transparency in Methods**: AI researchers should strive to be transparent about their research methods and results, sharing both the successes and limitations of their work with the broader scientific community and the public.

2. **Accountability in AI Research**:
   - o Researchers should be **accountable** for the ethical implications of their work. If an AI system developed through their research causes harm or is used in a way that infringes upon people's rights, researchers must take responsibility for their actions and be willing to engage in open discussions about the consequences of their work.
   - o **Example**: Researchers working on autonomous weapon systems or surveillance technologies must carefully consider the ethical ramifications of their work, particularly regarding potential misuse and societal harm.

3. **Collaboration with Policymakers and Ethicists**:
   - o AI researchers should collaborate with ethicists, policymakers, and other stakeholders to ensure that their work aligns with broader societal values and ethical standards. This includes engaging with those who may be affected by AI systems, such as vulnerable populations or marginalized communities, to ensure that the technology does not exacerbate inequalities or harm people.

Real-World Example: Ethical Dilemmas Faced by AI Researchers Working on Facial Recognition

Facial recognition technology, powered by AI, has faced significant ethical scrutiny due to its potential to infringe on privacy, promote surveillance, and exacerbate bias and discrimination. AI researchers working on facial recognition systems face several ethical dilemmas related to the use and deployment of this technology.

1. **Privacy Concerns**:
   - o One of the key ethical concerns with facial recognition technology is the **invasion of privacy**. AI researchers developing facial recognition systems may be asked to build systems that can track and identify individuals in public spaces without their consent. This raises

questions about the balance between security and individual privacy rights.

- o **Example**: Facial recognition systems deployed in public spaces or at border control points can track people's movements without their knowledge, creating a surveillance infrastructure that undermines privacy rights and freedom of movement.

2. **Bias and Discrimination**:

- o Facial recognition systems have been shown to exhibit significant biases, particularly when it comes to racial and gender differences. Studies have revealed that these systems are less accurate at identifying Black people, women, and people with non-European facial features, which can lead to **false positives** and **discriminatory outcomes**.

- o **Example**: Researchers working on facial recognition technologies may face pressure to improve the accuracy of these systems, but they must also confront the ethical dilemma of whether to prioritize technological progress over fairness. In some cases, the technology may reinforce racial profiling or discrimination, particularly when deployed in law enforcement or security contexts.

3. **Surveillance and Social Control**:

- o AI researchers developing facial recognition systems may also be confronted with the ethical implications of using this technology for **surveillance** or **social control**. In some countries, facial recognition is used in conjunction with government surveillance systems to monitor citizens, often without their knowledge or consent.

o **Example**: In **China**, facial recognition is widely used for surveillance, and AI researchers working on such technologies face ethical dilemmas regarding the use of their research to facilitate state-sponsored control over citizens' behavior. Researchers must decide whether their work could potentially be misused to infringe upon human rights.

4. **Balancing Innovation and Ethics**:
   o For AI researchers, balancing the pursuit of technological innovation with the **ethical considerations** of their work is a constant challenge. While advancements in facial recognition and AI offer significant benefits, such as improving security and convenience, they also carry risks of harm and abuse. Researchers must carefully weigh the potential benefits against the ethical costs and consider how their technology might be used by others once it is released.

Summary

In this chapter, we explored the **ethical challenges** in AI development, focusing on the role of **developers**, **researchers**, and other stakeholders in ensuring that AI technologies are created and deployed responsibly. We discussed how developers are responsible for embedding ethical principles such as **fairness**, **accountability**, and **transparency** into their AI systems and the importance of balancing technical, ethical, and business considerations.

We also highlighted the **responsibilities of AI researchers**, emphasizing their role in ensuring ethical research practices, minimizing bias, and collaborating with stakeholders to align AI development with societal values. The chapter concluded with a **real-world example** of the **ethical dilemmas faced by AI researchers working on facial recognition**, illustrating the tensions between innovation and the potential harm that AI technologies can cause if not developed responsibly.

As AI continues to evolve, it is crucial that those involved in its development and research remain committed to ethical standards that prioritize **human rights**, **fairness**, and **public good**, ensuring that AI technologies serve society in positive and responsible ways.

CHAPTER 18

The Role of AI in Human Rights

AI and Human Rights: The Impact of AI on Civil Liberties and Individual Rights

Artificial intelligence has the potential to significantly affect **human rights**, both positively and negatively. On the one hand, AI can be a powerful tool for promoting **civil liberties** and improving **individual rights**. On the other hand, the widespread use of AI also raises significant concerns about the erosion of **privacy**, **freedom of expression**, **due process**, and **equality**. AI systems, particularly those involved in surveillance, decision-making, and automation, can have far-reaching implications for fundamental human rights.

1. **Privacy and Surveillance**:
   o AI technologies such as facial recognition, predictive policing, and social media monitoring can be used to track individuals' movements, communications, and behaviors, often without their consent or knowledge. This can lead to **mass surveillance**, which infringes upon **privacy rights** and undermines civil liberties. When AI is used to monitor individuals in public spaces or in online environments, it can create a chilling effect on free speech and freedom of association.

o **Example**: The use of AI-powered surveillance cameras in public spaces, such as in China's **social credit system**, has raised concerns about constant monitoring and the erosion of privacy.

2. **Freedom of Expression and Autonomy**:
   o AI systems, particularly those deployed by governments or large corporations, can impact freedom of expression. Automated content moderation systems used by social media platforms can censor speech, potentially silencing dissent or minority viewpoints. AI algorithms that prioritize certain types of content—such as clickbait or sensational stories—can shape public discourse in ways that manipulate or distort public opinion.
   o **Example**: Content moderation algorithms on platforms like **Facebook** and **Twitter** may inadvertently silence individuals or groups, especially in authoritarian regimes where dissent is suppressed.

3. **Equality and Non-Discrimination**:
   o AI systems have the potential to perpetuate or even exacerbate existing **discrimination** in society. If AI systems are trained on biased data, they can reinforce inequalities based on race, gender, age, or socioeconomic status. This can lead to **discriminatory practices** in areas such as hiring, lending, healthcare, and law enforcement.

Ensuring that AI systems are designed to be fair and equitable is crucial for protecting human rights and promoting social justice.

o **Example**: In the criminal justice system, AI tools used for sentencing or parole decisions can replicate historical biases, leading to unfair treatment of certain racial or ethnic groups.

Protecting Human Rights in AI Systems: Designing AI Systems that Uphold Rights

As AI technologies evolve and become more embedded in society, it is essential to design and implement AI systems that prioritize **human rights**. AI must be developed with a commitment to protecting individual liberties, privacy, and freedom from discrimination. Developers and organizations must embed ethical principles into AI systems, ensuring that these technologies promote the **common good** and uphold **international human rights standards**.

1. **Privacy by Design**:
   o AI systems must be designed to **protect privacy** by minimizing the amount of personal data collected and ensuring that this data is only used for the purpose for which it was collected. Techniques like **data anonymization**, **encryption**, and **differential privacy** can help safeguard individuals' privacy rights.

- o **Data Minimization**: AI systems should collect the least amount of personal information necessary for their operation. This can help prevent the overreach of surveillance technologies and reduce the risk of data breaches.
- o **Example**: When developing facial recognition systems, developers must ensure that the data is collected with the consent of the individuals being monitored, and that the system cannot be used for mass surveillance without proper safeguards.

2. **Fairness and Accountability**:
   - o **Fairness**: AI systems must be **fair** and **non-discriminatory**. Developers must ensure that their systems do not disproportionately affect vulnerable or marginalized groups, and they should actively mitigate biases in the data and models used to train AI systems. Fairness can be achieved through techniques like **bias audits**, **adversarial testing**, and **diverse data collection**.
   - o **Accountability**: It must be clear who is responsible for AI systems, especially when these systems cause harm or violate human rights. Developers, companies, and governments must ensure that AI systems are **accountable** and that there are legal frameworks in place to address grievances and hold parties responsible for any abuses or violations.

- o **Example**: In AI-based hiring systems, companies should ensure that their algorithms do not favor certain genders, ethnicities, or other protected characteristics, which would violate anti-discrimination laws.

3. **Transparency and Explainability**:
   - o AI systems should be **transparent** and **explainable** to the public, especially when they are used in sensitive areas such as criminal justice, healthcare, and hiring. People should be able to understand how AI systems make decisions, and they should be informed about the data and processes used to make those decisions.
   - o **Example**: If an AI system used in a criminal justice setting recommends a prison sentence or parole decision, the individual affected should have the right to know how that decision was made and be able to challenge it if necessary.

4. **Ethical Guidelines and Governance**:
   - o AI development should be guided by **ethical frameworks** that prioritize human rights. Governments, industry groups, and international organizations should create and enforce regulations and guidelines that ensure AI systems respect individuals' rights. Additionally, AI systems should be regularly audited to ensure compliance with these ethical standards.

- o **Example**: The **OECD AI Principles** and the **EU AI Act** provide guidelines on how AI should be developed and deployed in ways that uphold human rights and ethical standards.

The Global Perspective on AI and Human Rights: International Efforts and Challenges

AI development and deployment have global implications for human rights, and there are a variety of international efforts to address the ethical challenges of AI. However, there are also significant challenges in achieving **global consensus** on how to regulate and govern AI technologies to ensure they align with **human rights**.

1. **International Human Rights Frameworks**:
   - o **United Nations**: The **United Nations** (UN) has emphasized the importance of protecting human rights in the context of AI. The **UN Declaration on Human Rights** and the **Universal Declaration of Bioethics and Human Rights** highlight the need to ensure that AI is developed in ways that respect human dignity, privacy, and autonomy.
   - o **OECD**: The **Organisation for Economic Co-operation and Development (OECD)** has established principles for AI that emphasize the need for fairness, accountability, and transparency. These guidelines aim to ensure that AI systems

are designed and deployed with human rights in mind.

2. **Challenges in Global Regulation**:
   o Different countries have different **regulatory approaches** to AI, making it challenging to develop universal standards for the protection of human rights. While some countries, such as the **EU,** have taken a proactive approach to AI governance, others, such as **China,** have adopted a more authoritarian approach that raises concerns about individual freedoms.
   o **Example**: In countries where AI is used for social control, such as China's use of AI in its **social credit system**, AI can infringe upon **individual freedoms** and **privacy**. In contrast, democratic nations are focused on ensuring AI respects civil liberties, but their regulations may not be as robust or as universally enforced.

3. **AI for Global Good**:
   o AI has the potential to contribute positively to **human rights** by improving access to education, healthcare, and economic opportunities. For example, AI-powered tools can help in identifying human trafficking victims, predicting natural disasters, or improving access to legal aid. The key challenge is to ensure that these AI applications do not inadvertently violate human rights in their deployment.

- o **Example**: AI is being used to improve **access to healthcare** in low-income regions by enabling remote diagnostics and treatment recommendations. However, ethical concerns arise when such systems fail to account for local cultural contexts or inadvertently exclude marginalized groups.

Real-World Example: AI in Refugee and Migrant Surveillance Systems

AI is increasingly used in **refugee and migrant surveillance** systems, raising significant ethical and human rights concerns. AI technologies such as facial recognition, biometric data collection, and predictive analytics are used to monitor and manage the movement of refugees and migrants across borders.

1. **AI in Border Control**:
   - o AI-powered systems are deployed at **border control points**, airports, and immigration offices to track and manage the flow of migrants and refugees. These systems are used to verify identities, monitor movements, and predict migration patterns. While these systems can enhance security, they also raise concerns about the rights of migrants and refugees, particularly in terms of **privacy** and **freedom of movement**.
2. **Surveillance and Profiling**:

- Facial recognition and biometric tracking systems are often used to identify individuals at border control points. These systems can help authorities monitor individuals who are crossing borders, but they also risk racial profiling, discrimination, and invasion of privacy.
- Example: In Europe, AI-driven systems are used to track migrants as they cross borders, often without their consent or knowledge. While these systems can provide security, they can also lead to the profiling and targeting of vulnerable populations, such as asylum seekers or refugees.

3. Ethical Concerns:
   - Invasion of Privacy: The use of AI to track refugees and migrants often involves the collection of sensitive personal data, which may be misused or exploited. Migrants, especially those fleeing conflict or persecution, may not have the opportunity to consent to the data collection, raising concerns about privacy violations and human dignity.
   - Freedom of Movement: AI surveillance systems that track migrant and refugee movements can restrict their freedom of movement and create barriers to seeking asylum or better living conditions. When migrants are constantly monitored, they may face limited opportunities for a fair

asylum process and be at risk of deportation or detention based on automated decisions made by AI systems.

Summary

In this chapter, we explored the intersection of **AI and human rights**, examining how AI systems impact **civil liberties** and **individual rights**. We discussed the potential **positive and negative consequences** of AI in areas such as **privacy, freedom of expression, equality**, and **non-discrimination**.

We also examined how to **protect human rights** in AI systems through the principles of **privacy by design, fairness, accountability**, and **transparency**. Ethical AI systems must prioritize individual rights and ensure that they do not disproportionately harm vulnerable or marginalized groups.

The chapter also covered the **global perspective** on AI and human rights, highlighting international efforts such as those from the **UN** and **OECD**, as well as the challenges in achieving a **global consensus** on AI governance.

Finally, we discussed a **real-world example** of **AI in refugee and migrant surveillance systems**, illustrating the ethical concerns surrounding the use of AI to monitor and control migrant populations. These systems raise significant questions about privacy, freedom of movement, and human dignity, underscoring the importance of designing AI systems that protect human rights.

As AI continues to shape society, it is essential that these technologies are developed and deployed in ways that uphold the fundamental rights of all individuals, ensuring that they serve the common good without infringing on personal freedoms or dignity.

CHAPTER 19

Bias Detection and Mitigation

How to Detect Bias: Tools and Techniques for Identifying Bias in AI Models

Bias in AI models can arise from various sources, including biased data, flawed algorithms, and skewed assumptions made during development. Detecting bias early in the AI development process is crucial for ensuring that the system performs fairly and does not perpetuate or amplify existing inequalities.

1. **Data Exploration and Analysis**:
    o **Examine the Data**: Bias often originates from the data used to train AI models. It's essential to analyze the data for potential imbalances or underrepresentation of certain groups. For example, in a facial recognition system, if the dataset contains more images of lighter-skinned individuals than darker-skinned individuals, the model will likely perform less accurately for people of color.
    o **Data Audits**: Data audits involve systematically reviewing datasets to check for patterns of inequality or exclusion. This includes checking for racial, gender, age, or socioeconomic biases in the data.
    o **Example**: A dataset used for training a hiring algorithm might over-represent

candidates from certain demographic groups (e.g., white male applicants) while under-representing others (e.g., women or people of color). Identifying such imbalances in the dataset is the first step in detecting bias.

2. **Bias Detection Tools**:

   o **Fairness Indicators**: Tools like **IBM AI Fairness 360**, **Google's Fairness Indicators**, and **Fairness Flow** can help detect bias in AI models by evaluating how well a model performs across different demographic groups. These tools provide metrics such as **demographic parity** and **equalized odds** to identify disparities in the model's outcomes.

   o **Model Auditing**: Auditing the model's output across different demographic groups can reveal whether certain groups are being unfairly impacted. This can include checking for disparities in accuracy, error rates, or other performance metrics for different populations.

   o **Explainability Tools**: Explainable AI (XAI) tools such as **LIME** (Local Interpretable Model-Agnostic Explanations) and **SHAP** (SHapley Additive exPlanations) can be used to interpret model decisions and assess whether the model's reasoning is biased or discriminatory.

3. **Bias Testing Frameworks**:
   - ○ Establishing frameworks for testing AI models for bias is an essential step in ensuring fairness. For example, using **cross-validation** on different subsets of the data (e.g., by gender, race, or other protected attributes) can help detect any bias in the model's predictions across diverse groups.
   - ○ **Example**: Testing an AI system that makes loan approval decisions by evaluating its predictions across different racial groups to ensure that no group is unfairly denied credit.

Mitigating Bias: Practical Methods for Reducing Bias During Model Training

Once bias is detected, it is essential to mitigate it to ensure the AI model is fair and equitable. Several techniques can be employed during the model training process to reduce bias and enhance fairness.

1. **Bias Mitigation in Data**:
   - ○ **Rebalancing the Dataset**: One common method to reduce bias is to adjust the dataset to ensure that it is more representative of all groups. This can be done by **oversampling** underrepresented groups or **undersampling** overrepresented groups. Additionally, techniques like **data augmentation** can

generate more diverse examples for underrepresented groups.

- o **Data Preprocessing**: Before training a model, it's important to preprocess the data to ensure it doesn't include biased features or attributes. For example, removing or transforming sensitive features such as race or gender may help to reduce bias in certain cases.
- o **Example**: In a hiring algorithm, ensuring that the data is balanced in terms of gender and ethnicity can prevent the model from learning gender or racial biases.

2. **Bias Mitigation during Model Training**:
   - o **Fairness Constraints**: When training AI models, fairness constraints can be applied to ensure that the model's decisions do not disproportionately affect specific groups. These constraints can be added to the training process as an optimization objective, ensuring that the model is not only accurate but also fair.
   - o **Adversarial Training**: In adversarial training, an additional model (the adversary) is trained to detect and counteract bias in the primary model. The goal is for the primary model to learn features that do not correlate with sensitive attributes (e.g., race, gender) while still performing the task effectively.
   - o **Example**: In a predictive policing model, adversarial training could help ensure that

the model does not rely on factors such as race, which could inadvertently lead to biased law enforcement practices.

3. **Regularization Techniques**:
   - o **Regularization** methods such as **L1** and **L2 regularization** can help prevent the model from fitting too closely to the data, which can inadvertently amplify biases. Regularization helps generalize the model and prevents overfitting to biased patterns present in the training data.
   - o **Fair Representation Learning**: This approach involves training the AI model to learn representations of data that are **fair** and unbiased, ensuring that sensitive attributes (e.g., race, gender) are not disproportionately influencing the model's predictions.

4. **Continuous Monitoring and Retraining**:
   - o **Post-deployment monitoring** is necessary to ensure that the AI model continues to perform fairly as new data is introduced. AI models can drift over time, and new biases may emerge as the system encounters new data. Continuous monitoring and periodic retraining help to identify and mitigate bias in evolving datasets.
   - o **Example**: A hiring algorithm that initially performs well may start showing bias if societal trends change, such as shifts in gender or racial representation in certain job fields. Monitoring the model and

retraining it with new, diverse data ensures that it remains fair.

Building Bias-Resilient Systems: Best Practices for Creating Fair and Unbiased AI

Creating AI systems that are **bias-resilient** and fair requires a holistic approach that integrates fairness into every phase of development, from data collection to model deployment. The following best practices can help ensure that AI systems are both fair and ethical.

1. **Diverse and Inclusive Teams**:
   o Diversity among the development team is critical in identifying and mitigating bias. A team with diverse perspectives, backgrounds, and experiences is more likely to recognize potential biases in the data or model and address them effectively. Including ethicists, sociologists, and individuals from affected communities in the development process can provide valuable insights into potential social impacts.
   o **Example**: A diverse team working on a healthcare AI system can better identify biases related to race, gender, or socioeconomic status, ensuring that the model works equitably across all demographics.
2. **Stakeholder Involvement**:
   o Engaging with stakeholders—especially those who will be affected by AI

systems—can help ensure that the system meets ethical standards. Stakeholder involvement can include consulting affected communities, conducting focus groups, and gathering feedback throughout the development and deployment stages.

- o **Example**: Before deploying a predictive policing system, law enforcement agencies could engage with local communities to understand concerns and ensure that the system is not disproportionately targeting minority neighborhoods.

3. **Ethical Auditing and Impact Assessments**:
   - o Ethical audits and **impact assessments** should be conducted regularly to identify any unintended consequences or biases in AI systems. These audits should be transparent and include independent third parties to assess the fairness of the system. Ethical audits should focus on the **transparency**, **accountability**, and **impact** of AI systems, ensuring that they do not harm individuals or communities.
   - o **Example**: A financial institution deploying an AI-driven credit scoring model should perform regular audits to ensure that the model does not unfairly disadvantage certain racial or ethnic groups in terms of loan approval.

4. **Feedback Mechanisms**:

- o AI systems should be designed with **feedback loops** that allow users to report errors or issues. This is particularly important in high-stakes areas like hiring, healthcare, or criminal justice, where biased decisions can have significant consequences for individuals.
- o **Example**: A job application AI system should allow applicants to appeal decisions and flag potential biases in the system's outputs. This helps ensure that the system remains fair and equitable over time.

Real-World Example: Mitigating Bias in AI-Powered Hiring Tools

AI-powered hiring tools have become increasingly common in the recruitment process, helping organizations filter resumes, assess candidates, and make hiring decisions. However, these systems are at risk of perpetuating existing biases in the hiring process, leading to discrimination based on race, gender, or other protected characteristics.

1. **Bias in Hiring Algorithms**:
   - o AI-powered hiring tools are often trained on historical data, which can include biased patterns such as gender or racial discrimination in previous hiring decisions. If these biases are not addressed, the AI system can inadvertently favor certain groups over

others, leading to discriminatory outcomes.

- o **Example**: In 2018, Amazon scrapped an AI-driven recruitment tool after discovering that it was biased against female candidates. The tool was trained on resumes submitted to Amazon over a 10-year period, which predominantly came from male applicants. As a result, the system favored male candidates and penalized female applicants.

2. **Mitigating Bias in Hiring Tools**:
   - o **Data Rebalancing**: To mitigate bias, companies can use more diverse datasets that reflect the full range of candidates, ensuring that the training data includes equal representation from all gender, racial, and ethnic groups.
   - o **Bias Audits and Testing**: Companies can perform regular **bias audits** to evaluate the fairness of their hiring algorithms. These audits check for any discriminatory outcomes and ensure that the system treats all candidates equitably.
   - o **Transparency and Feedback**: Companies can provide transparency in their hiring algorithms, explaining how decisions are made and allowing candidates to receive feedback on their application status. Additionally, feedback mechanisms can be implemented to help candidates challenge potentially biased decisions.

3. **Ethical Frameworks for Hiring AI**:
   - AI-powered hiring systems should be developed in accordance with **ethical frameworks** that prioritize fairness, transparency, and accountability. This includes ensuring that the AI model is continuously updated to reflect societal changes and that it does not unintentionally perpetuate historical biases.
   - **Example**: Companies like **HireVue** are working on improving their AI hiring systems by incorporating ethical standards, focusing on fairness, and using diverse datasets to prevent bias in the recruitment process.

Summary

In this chapter, we explored **bias detection** and **mitigation** in AI, focusing on the tools and techniques available to identify and reduce bias in AI models. We discussed the importance of detecting bias in data, using fairness metrics, and auditing model performance to ensure that AI systems are fair and equitable.

We also outlined practical methods for **mitigating bias** during model training, including data rebalancing, bias constraints, adversarial training, and continuous monitoring. Additionally, we explored best practices for **building bias-resilient systems**, emphasizing the need for diverse teams, stakeholder involvement, and ethical auditing.

The chapter concluded with a **real-world example** of **mitigating bias in AI-powered hiring tools**, highlighting the importance of transparency, fairness, and accountability in AI recruitment systems. By following these practices, we can ensure that AI systems are designed to be **fair**, **non-discriminatory**, and **accountable** in their decision-making, ultimately promoting a more equitable and just society.

CHAPTER 20

Transparency in AI Algorithms

What is Algorithmic Transparency?: The Importance of Transparency in AI Systems

Algorithmic transparency refers to the ability to understand and explain how AI systems make decisions. As AI becomes increasingly integrated into society, from **healthcare** to **finance** to **criminal justice**, ensuring that AI systems are transparent is vital for building trust, accountability, and fairness. Without transparency, AI models can become **black boxes**, where their inner workings are opaque and difficult for users, regulators, or even the developers themselves to understand.

1. **Trust and Accountability**:
   o Transparency ensures that AI systems are not only accurate but also **accountable**. If an AI model makes a decision that negatively impacts an individual— whether in hiring, healthcare, or finance—transparency allows the affected individual to understand how and why the decision was made. This transparency is essential for addressing concerns and ensuring that AI systems do not operate arbitrarily or unfairly.
   o **Example**: In the case of AI-powered hiring tools, transparency helps job applicants understand why they were

rejected, which can provide valuable feedback and help prevent discrimination.

2. **Fairness and Non-Discrimination**:
   - Transparency is key to identifying and addressing biases in AI systems. Without transparency, it is difficult to detect when a model is making biased or discriminatory decisions. By making AI systems more interpretable, developers and users can spot potential biases and take corrective actions.
   - **Example**: In predictive policing, algorithmic transparency is essential to ensure that AI systems are not unfairly targeting certain communities, particularly marginalized or minority groups.

3. **Legal and Ethical Compliance**:
   - Many regulations and ethical standards now require AI systems to be transparent. For instance, the **General Data Protection Regulation (GDPR)** in the European Union includes provisions for the **right to explanation**, which gives individuals the right to know how automated decisions are made about them.
   - **Example**: GDPR mandates that if a person is subject to a decision made by an AI system (e.g., credit scoring or hiring decisions), they must have access to an explanation of the logic behind that decision.

Making AI Models Interpretable: Methods to Explain Complex Models

Many modern AI systems, particularly those based on deep learning and neural networks, are often seen as "black boxes" due to their complexity. While these models may perform extremely well in terms of accuracy, their lack of interpretability makes it challenging for users and developers to understand why the model arrived at a particular decision.

1. **Interpretable Models**:
   o **Simple Models**: One approach to achieving transparency is to use simpler models that are more interpretable by design, such as **decision trees** or **linear regression models**. These models have a straightforward structure, making it easier to trace how input features affect the output decision.
   o **Example**: A decision tree model used to predict whether a loan application should be approved can be more easily understood than a deep neural network model. The decisions are based on clear rules such as "approve if income > $50,000" or "deny if credit score < 600."
2. **Model-Agnostic Interpretation Methods**:
   o **LIME (Local Interpretable Model-Agnostic Explanations)**: LIME is a popular technique used to interpret complex models. It works by approximating a black-box model locally

(i.e., around a specific prediction) using a simpler, interpretable model. This allows developers to understand how the model is making predictions for individual data points.

o **SHAP (SHapley Additive exPlanations)**: SHAP is another powerful method for explaining AI models, particularly those used in machine learning. SHAP values break down a prediction into contributions from each feature, providing a clear understanding of how each feature influences the model's decision.

o **Example**: In a credit scoring model, SHAP values could show that a customer's **credit history** contributed +0.4 to the decision, while their **age** contributed -0.1, helping explain why a particular loan decision was made.

3. **Visualizations for Interpretability**:
   o **Feature Importance**: One way to enhance the transparency of AI models is to visualize which features are most important in making decisions. Tools like **feature importance plots** and **partial dependence plots** help developers and users understand which variables are influencing predictions and how they impact the outcome.
   o **Activation Maps**: In deep learning, particularly for image recognition tasks, activation maps can show which parts of

an image are most important for a model's decision. These maps help users understand what the model is "looking at" to make predictions.

- o **Example**: In a medical AI system used for diagnosing X-rays, activation maps might highlight areas of an image where the AI focuses on detecting abnormalities, such as lung nodules.

Ensuring Openness: Sharing Models and Algorithms Responsibly

Ensuring transparency in AI systems also involves **openness**—the sharing of models, algorithms, and data in a way that promotes trust and accountability. However, the sharing of AI systems must be done responsibly, balancing transparency with concerns about security, privacy, and intellectual property.

1. **Open-Source AI Models**:
   - o Sharing AI models as **open-source software** allows other developers, researchers, and organizations to scrutinize, modify, and improve the model. This helps ensure that the model is being used ethically and that any potential flaws or biases are addressed by the community.
   - o **Example**: Open-source machine learning libraries like **TensorFlow** and **PyTorch** allow developers to understand how AI models work, modify them for specific

use cases, and identify any unintended consequences of their design.

2. **Responsible Data Sharing**:
   o Sharing data used to train AI models is a crucial part of ensuring transparency. However, sharing sensitive data must be done responsibly, with adequate privacy protections in place. For instance, data can be anonymized to prevent the identification of individuals, and shared under strict terms and conditions to ensure it is used ethically.
   o **Example**: The **OpenAI GPT-3** model has been made available to the public through a controlled API, allowing researchers and developers to use the model while mitigating risks related to abuse or misuse.

3. **Third-Party Audits and Certifications**:
   o Independent audits and certifications can provide assurance that AI models are transparent and comply with ethical guidelines. Third-party audits help ensure that the AI systems are not only functioning as intended but also adhering to legal and ethical standards regarding fairness, privacy, and accountability.
   o **Example**: Certification schemes like **IEEE's Global Initiative on Ethics of Autonomous and Intelligent Systems** or **ISO 9001** can provide an external, unbiased review of AI systems, ensuring

that transparency and ethical standards are met.

4. **Clear Communication with Stakeholders**:
   - It's important that developers and organizations clearly communicate the workings of their AI models to **stakeholders**, including users, regulators, and the general public. Transparent documentation should explain how the model was trained, the data used, the algorithms involved, and any potential limitations or risks associated with the system.
   - **Example**: In healthcare, AI systems used to recommend treatments or diagnose diseases should be accompanied by detailed documentation that explains how the model makes its decisions, what data it was trained on, and any potential risks involved in using it.

Real-World Example: Transparency in AI Used in Healthcare Decision-Making

AI is increasingly being deployed in healthcare settings to assist in decision-making, from diagnosing diseases to recommending treatments. However, transparency in these AI systems is crucial, as they directly impact people's health and well-being. Without transparency, patients and healthcare professionals may be unable to trust the AI's recommendations or understand why certain decisions were made.

1. **AI in Medical Diagnostics**:
   - AI systems, particularly in medical imaging, are used to assist radiologists in diagnosing conditions such as cancer, fractures, or heart disease. These systems can analyze X-rays, MRIs, and CT scans with impressive accuracy. However, for clinicians to trust the AI's results, the system must be transparent in how it makes its decisions.
   - **Example**: Google's **DeepMind** developed an AI system that can diagnose eye diseases from retinal scans. The system has been shown to perform as well as, or better than, human doctors in some cases. However, it is crucial for the system to explain the reasoning behind its diagnosis. For instance, if the system suggests a diagnosis of diabetic retinopathy, the AI model should provide information about the key features it identified in the scan that led to this conclusion.

2. **Ensuring Explainability**:
   - In healthcare, it's not enough for AI systems to just provide a diagnosis—they must also be explainable. Doctors and patients must be able to understand why a certain decision was made. Explainable AI techniques such as **LIME** and **SHAP** can help make medical AI systems interpretable by breaking down complex predictions and showing the most

important factors that influenced the decision.

- o **Example**: In a case where an AI system recommends a certain treatment for cancer, it should be able to explain why this treatment was selected, what data was used, and what factors contributed to the recommendation, so that doctors can make informed decisions in conjunction with the AI's suggestions.

3. **Regulatory Transparency**:
   - o Given the high stakes in healthcare, regulatory bodies like the **FDA** (Food and Drug Administration) in the U.S. have strict guidelines for the transparency of AI systems used in medical decision-making. AI models must undergo rigorous testing and validation, and companies must provide transparent reports on how their models are trained and how they perform.
   - o **Example**: For AI systems used in diagnosing medical conditions, companies must disclose the data used for training, how the AI was validated, and the potential risks associated with using the system, ensuring that healthcare professionals and patients can trust and understand the AI's decisions.

Summary

In this chapter, we explored the importance of **algorithmic transparency** in AI systems, emphasizing its role in building trust, accountability, and fairness. We discussed how to **make AI models interpretable** through various methods such as **LIME, SHAP**, and simple models, as well as the importance of **responsibly sharing models and algorithms** to ensure openness.

The chapter also included a **real-world example** of **transparency in AI used in healthcare decision-making**, highlighting the need for explainable AI in medical diagnostics and treatment recommendations. By making AI systems more transparent, explainable, and accountable, we can ensure that they are used ethically, effectively, and in ways that promote trust and equity.

As AI becomes increasingly integrated into sensitive areas like healthcare, finance, and criminal justice, ensuring that these systems are transparent will be essential to their successful and ethical implementation. Transparency fosters trust and accountability, helping to ensure that AI benefits society in a responsible and equitable way.

CHAPTER 21

AI and Global Governance

Global Coordination for AI Ethics: Why International Cooperation is Crucial

As artificial intelligence rapidly evolves and spreads across the globe, the need for **international cooperation** in AI governance has never been more critical. AI has a **transnational impact**, affecting everything from economic structures and labor markets to privacy rights and national security. Because AI systems are increasingly used in global contexts, the ethical and regulatory challenges they present are also global in nature, requiring a unified approach.

1. **AI's Cross-Border Impact**:
   o AI technologies do not adhere to national borders, and their implications transcend local laws and regulations. AI systems used in areas like **healthcare**, **surveillance**, **financial markets**, and **military applications** can easily span across countries and regions, making global governance essential for addressing issues such as **privacy** violations, **cybersecurity** risks, and **human rights** abuses.
   o **Example**: An AI-powered surveillance system developed in one country can be deployed globally, impacting privacy rights in multiple countries, regardless of

whether those nations have their own data protection laws in place.

2. **Collective Action for Ethical Standards**:
   o Global coordination can help establish **shared ethical principles** for AI development and deployment, ensuring that AI technologies are used for the benefit of humanity and do not exacerbate existing inequalities or infringe on basic rights. Collective action can also help ensure that AI systems are used transparently and fairly, preventing exploitation and minimizing risks.
   o **Example**: AI systems in **autonomous vehicles** have the potential to save lives, but also pose ethical dilemmas (e.g., in crash scenarios). Global coordination can help establish consistent safety and ethical standards for AI deployment in this area.

3. **Addressing Global Power Imbalances**:
   o As AI technology becomes a central driver of economic and political power, it is essential that its benefits are **equitably distributed**. Countries with advanced AI capabilities can dominate global markets, leaving developing countries behind. International cooperation is necessary to ensure that **AI does not exacerbate global inequalities** but instead serves as a tool for addressing global challenges such as **poverty**, **healthcare access**, and **climate change**.

○ **Example**: While advanced AI models have been developed by companies in high-income countries, **low-income nations** often lack the infrastructure, expertise, and data access needed to benefit from AI technologies. International cooperation can help bridge this gap.

Building Global AI Governance Frameworks: Global Standards for AI Ethics and Accountability

For AI to develop responsibly and ethically on a global scale, **global AI governance frameworks** are essential. These frameworks should be designed to create standards for AI ethics, accountability, and transparency that are universally recognized and respected, regardless of a country's level of technological development.

1. **Developing Universal Ethical Guidelines**:
   ○ International organizations and governmental bodies must work together to establish **universal ethical guidelines** for AI. These guidelines should encompass a wide range of issues, including **fairness**, **accountability**, **privacy**, and **safety**. AI models should be held to high standards, ensuring that they respect human rights and contribute to the well-being of all people.
   ○ **Example**: The **OECD's Principles on Artificial Intelligence** provide a

framework for developing and deploying AI that respects human rights, fairness, and accountability. These principles can serve as a baseline for creating more detailed regulatory frameworks and agreements.

2. **Global AI Regulation**:
   - Governments and international bodies must establish regulatory systems that ensure that AI technologies are **accountable** and **transparent**. These regulations can help prevent misuse, ensure data protection, and hold developers and companies accountable for the impact of their AI systems. International cooperation is necessary to create regulatory frameworks that are consistent across borders, addressing cross-national concerns like **privacy**, **security**, and **human rights**.
   - **Example**: The **EU's AI Act** is a pioneering effort to regulate AI with a focus on risk-based regulation. It aims to create clear guidelines for AI applications based on their potential impact on individuals and society.

3. **International Collaboration on AI Research and Development**:
   - Collaboration between countries and regions is also essential for ensuring that AI research and development is conducted **ethically** and that it benefits the global community. Collaborative

international research initiatives can address global challenges like **climate change**, **healthcare**, and **education**, while ensuring that AI models do not disproportionately benefit certain groups at the expense of others.

- o **Example**: The **Global Partnership on Artificial Intelligence (GPAI)** is an initiative involving various countries and regions to promote the responsible development and use of AI. GPAI brings together governments, academia, and industry to share research and best practices for AI development.

4. **Incentivizing Global Cooperation**:
- o Governments and organizations can also use incentives, such as funding for ethical AI research, international collaborations, and knowledge-sharing ·platforms, to encourage global cooperation. These incentives can help align AI development with the **public good** and prevent AI from being misused for harmful purposes.
- o **Example**: The **World Economic Forum (WEF)** has developed initiatives to promote **AI for good**, encouraging governments, organizations, and researchers to collaborate on AI projects that address global challenges, such as hunger and disease.

Ensuring Fairness in a Global Context: Addressing Disparities in AI Access and Impact

While AI has the potential to improve lives across the world, there are significant disparities in **access** to AI technologies and the **impact** of these systems on different populations. Ensuring fairness in a global context means addressing these disparities and making sure that AI benefits all people, regardless of where they live or their socioeconomic status.

1. **Bridging the Digital Divide**:
   o The global **digital divide**—the gap between regions with access to technology and those without—poses a significant challenge for ensuring fairness in AI. Countries in the **Global South** often lack the infrastructure, data, and computational resources needed to develop and benefit from AI. International cooperation is essential to bridge this gap and promote **AI inclusivity** by providing the necessary resources, education, and support to underdeveloped regions.
   o **Example**: Initiatives like **AI for Good**, supported by organizations such as the **UN** and **GPAI**, aim to provide AI solutions that are accessible to low-income countries and ensure that these countries can participate in and benefit from AI development.

2. **Addressing Bias and Discrimination in Global AI Systems**:
    o AI systems often reflect the biases present in the data used to train them. These biases can disproportionately affect vulnerable or marginalized groups, especially in global contexts where datasets may not fully represent diverse populations. Ensuring fairness in global AI systems requires actively addressing these biases, such as by using diverse and representative datasets and developing **bias mitigation techniques**.
    o **Example**: A global AI model used for healthcare may perform poorly in some regions due to the lack of diverse data representing specific populations. International collaboration can help address this by ensuring that AI models are trained on more inclusive datasets.

3. **AI as a Tool for Social Justice**:
    o AI can be a powerful tool for addressing **global inequalities** and advancing **social justice**. By deploying AI to tackle issues such as **poverty**, **healthcare access**, and **education**, governments and international organizations can harness AI to improve lives, especially in underserved regions.
    o **Example**: AI can be used to improve healthcare delivery in low-resource settings by enabling telemedicine, diagnostics, and resource allocation in

real-time. However, this requires addressing challenges such as access to data, technology infrastructure, and training for healthcare workers.

4. **Ensuring Fair Access to AI Technologies**:
   o Fair access to AI technologies also includes addressing the issue of **intellectual property**. In some regions, AI technology is owned and controlled by a few large companies, leading to an uneven distribution of knowledge and technology. International collaboration can ensure that AI knowledge is shared fairly, fostering innovation and growth in developing countries.
   o **Example**: Collaborative AI research efforts that pool resources and expertise from multiple countries can ensure that developing nations have access to cutting-edge AI technologies that they may not have the resources to develop on their own.

Real-World Example: The Role of the United Nations in AI Governance Discussions

The **United Nations (UN)** plays a crucial role in promoting global cooperation and establishing international standards for the development and deployment of AI. The UN has recognized AI's potential to both benefit and harm global society, and it has actively engaged in discussions about AI governance and ethics to ensure that AI technologies align with international human rights standards.

1. **The UN's AI for Good Initiative**:
   o The **UN's AI for Good** initiative is a global effort to use AI to achieve the **Sustainable Development Goals (SDGs)**, such as ending poverty, achieving gender equality, and addressing climate change. AI for Good focuses on ensuring that AI serves humanity and advances social justice, particularly for marginalized communities.
   o **Example**: AI for Good projects include AI-driven solutions for healthcare, education, disaster response, and environmental protection. The initiative fosters global collaboration among governments, businesses, and non-governmental organizations (NGOs) to create sustainable and equitable AI applications.

2. **The UN's Role in AI Ethics**:
   o The UN has also taken an active role in addressing the ethical implications of AI. Through bodies such as the **UNESCO** (United Nations Educational, Scientific and Cultural Organization), the UN has developed guidelines and frameworks for the ethical use of AI. The **UNESCO Recommendation on the Ethics of AI** outlines key principles such as human

dignity, privacy, transparency, and accountability.
- o **Example**: In 2021, UNESCO released a **global framework for the ethics of artificial intelligence**, emphasizing the importance of protecting human rights, ensuring AI is used for the public good, and promoting inclusivity.
3. **Addressing AI in Global Security**:
- o The UN has also addressed the risks of AI in the context of **global security**, especially as AI technologies are increasingly used in military applications, cybersecurity, and surveillance. Discussions at the UN focus on regulating the use of AI in military systems, such as **autonomous weapons**, to ensure that AI is not used to perpetrate violence or conflict.
- o **Example**: The UN's efforts in regulating **autonomous weapons systems** aim to ensure that AI is used responsibly in the military, preventing the development of fully autonomous weapons that can act without human intervention.

Summary

In this chapter, we explored the critical role of **global governance** in ensuring that AI is developed and deployed ethically, equitably, and responsibly. We discussed the need for **international cooperation** in AI ethics and regulation, emphasizing the importance of **shared standards** for AI development, as well as the need to address **disparities in AI access and impact** across different countries and regions.

We examined how **global AI governance frameworks** can ensure fairness, transparency, and accountability in AI systems, and highlighted the **United Nations' role** in fostering international discussions on AI ethics, including its efforts to promote AI for social good and ensure AI's alignment with human rights standards.

As AI continues to influence every facet of global society, it is essential that countries and organizations work together to create a cohesive and just framework for AI governance that benefits everyone and ensures that the technology serves the common good.

CHAPTER 22

The Impact of AI on Democracy

AI's Influence on Elections: Social Media, Misinformation, and Targeted Ads

AI has dramatically changed the landscape of politics, particularly in the context of **elections**. The ability of AI systems to process vast amounts of data and target individuals with personalized content has introduced new challenges and risks for democratic processes. AI-powered tools are now used extensively in political campaigning, primarily through **social media**, where algorithms influence public discourse and voter behavior.

1. **Social Media Algorithms and Political Discourse**:
   o Social media platforms like **Facebook, Twitter**, and **Instagram** use AI algorithms to curate content, recommending posts that align with users' past behaviors and preferences. While this personalization can enhance user engagement, it can also amplify **polarizing content** and **echo chambers**, where individuals are exposed primarily to information that reinforces their existing beliefs.
   o **Example**: During election cycles, social media platforms can inadvertently reinforce political biases, leading to a

fragmented public sphere where voters are not exposed to diverse perspectives or balanced information.

2. **Misinformation and Fake News**:
   o AI-driven tools can also be used to **generate and spread misinformation**. **Deepfakes**, AI-generated videos or audio clips that manipulate reality, and **bots** that flood social media with false information are prime examples of how AI can undermine democratic processes. These tools can be used to deceive voters, influence opinions, and distort public perceptions, often with significant consequences.
   o **Example**: In the **2016 U.S. presidential election**, AI-powered bots and fake news were heavily used to sway voters, with false information being deliberately spread across social media platforms.

3. **Targeted Political Ads**:
   o AI enables **hyper-targeted advertising** that can be used to manipulate public opinion. By analyzing personal data such as voting history, location, demographics, and online behavior, political campaigns can deliver tailored ads designed to influence individuals' voting decisions. These ads can be highly persuasive, even if they are misleading or inaccurate.
   o **Example**: During elections, political parties can use AI to micro-target voters with specific messages designed to sway

their vote, often without their full awareness of the manipulation happening behind the scenes.

Ensuring Fair Use of AI in Politics: Protecting Democratic Integrity

To ensure that AI serves democratic principles rather than undermining them, **regulations and frameworks** must be put in place to govern the use of AI in political campaigns. These safeguards must address issues related to **data privacy, transparency, accountability,** and **the prevention of manipulation**.

1. **Transparency in Political Campaigns**:
   o Political campaigns should be required to disclose when AI is being used to influence voters, whether through targeted ads, social media bots, or personalized content. Transparency is critical for ensuring that voters can make informed decisions about the information they are exposed to.
   o **Example**: Social media platforms like Facebook and Twitter have faced pressure to disclose the origins and intentions behind political ads. Implementing more robust policies for disclosing AI-driven political advertising is essential for ensuring transparency.
2. **Regulating Political AI**:
   o Governments and international organizations should establish clear rules

for the **ethical use** of AI in political campaigns. This includes regulating how personal data is collected and used, ensuring that political ads are **truthful**, and preventing the use of AI to **exploit vulnerabilities** in voters. AI systems should be audited for fairness and transparency before they are allowed to influence political discourse.

- o **Example**: The **General Data Protection Regulation (GDPR)** in Europe includes provisions that could apply to political campaigns, such as data consent and transparency requirements for political data collection.

3. **Public Awareness and Education**:
   - o Voters must be educated about the ways AI can influence elections and the potential for manipulation. This involves providing citizens with the tools to critically evaluate the content they encounter online and understand how algorithms might be shaping their political perceptions.
   - o **Example**: Governments and civic organizations can launch campaigns to raise awareness about **deepfakes**, fake news, and targeted political ads, teaching citizens to recognize signs of manipulation.

4. **Ensuring Data Privacy**:
   - o **Data privacy** must be prioritized in political AI applications. Voter data

should be protected, and any data collection by political campaigns should be transparent and consensual. Political campaigns should not be allowed to exploit private data to unduly influence voters or gain an unfair advantage in the electoral process.

- o **Example**: AI-driven campaigns should be required to gain explicit consent from voters before collecting personal data or targeting them with ads.

AI and Political Manipulation: Preventing AI-Driven Manipulation of Public Opinion

The manipulation of public opinion through AI is a serious threat to democratic integrity. When political entities use AI tools to manipulate voters—whether through spreading **misinformation, polarization**, or **targeted manipulation**—the very foundation of democratic processes is at risk.

1. **Combatting AI-Generated Misinformation**:
   - o One of the most significant challenges in preventing political manipulation is combating **AI-generated misinformation**. AI-powered tools can create **fake news** and **deepfakes** that are difficult to detect and debunk, spreading false or misleading information quickly. Social media platforms need to implement **AI detection tools** to identify

and stop the spread of harmful, manipulated content.

- ○ **Example**: **Deepfakes**—videos or audio recordings that are altered using AI—can be used to fabricate speeches or events that never happened, misleading voters into believing false narratives. AI tools that can detect deepfakes are crucial for preventing this type of manipulation.

2. **Regulating Political Bots**:

- ○ AI-driven **bots** can be used to flood social media platforms with **misleading information**, distorting public opinion by creating the illusion of broad support or opposition for a political cause. These bots can amplify divisive content, making it seem more popular than it actually is.

- ○ **Example**: Political campaigns or state actors may deploy thousands of bots to manipulate trends on platforms like Twitter or Facebook, making certain hashtags or topics go viral. Regulation should mandate transparency and prevent the use of bots to mislead voters.

3. **Algorithmic Transparency**:

- ○ AI algorithms that are used to manipulate public opinion must be **transparent** and **auditable**. Political campaigns should be required to disclose the use of AI in shaping their digital strategies, and they should be held accountable for the outcomes of such campaigns.

- Example: If a political party uses an AI algorithm to determine which messages to target to specific voter segments, they should disclose how those decisions were made and ensure that the algorithm does not unduly influence public opinion with biased or false information.
4. **Building Ethical AI for Political Campaigns**:
    - Ethical AI frameworks must be developed to guide political campaigns in the use of AI. These frameworks should address issues such as **bias**, **misleading advertising**, and the use of AI for **political manipulation**. By promoting **ethical AI use**, we can help ensure that AI enhances democracy rather than undermining it.
    - **Example**: Political campaigns could work with third-party auditors to assess the ethical implications of their AI-driven strategies, ensuring that they comply with ethical standards and do not manipulate or deceive voters.

Real-World Example: The Use of AI in Political Campaigning and Its Ethical Concerns

AI has already been used in political campaigns to influence voter behavior through targeted ads, personalized messaging, and social media manipulation. One of the most well-known cases of AI's impact on political campaigns was the use of

Cambridge Analytica during the **2016 U.S. presidential election**.

1. **Cambridge Analytica Scandal**:
   o **Cambridge Analytica**, a political consulting firm, used **Facebook data** to create psychological profiles of millions of American voters. This data was then used to target voters with personalized political ads that were designed to influence their behavior and sway their vote. The scandal highlighted the potential for AI and big data to manipulate voters on a massive scale without their knowledge or consent.
   o **Ethical Concerns**: The use of personal data without consent, along with the targeting of voters with personalized political messaging, raised significant ethical questions about privacy, transparency, and manipulation. In this case, AI was used to exploit personal data to sway elections, which many argue is a violation of democratic integrity.
2. **AI in Campaign Advertising**:
   o Political campaigns are increasingly using AI to optimize **ad placements** and craft tailored messages that resonate with specific voter groups. While this can make campaigns more efficient, it also raises concerns about the fairness of such targeted strategies and the potential for AI

to create **filter bubbles** that reinforce existing biases.

- o **Example**: AI-driven political ads, particularly during **Brexit** and the **2016 U.S. presidential election**, used data on voter preferences to tailor messages that appealed to voters' emotions and fears, often with misleading or false information. These ads can influence voters without giving them a fair or informed perspective.

3. **The Importance of Regulation**:
   - o The ethical concerns raised by the use of AI in political campaigns underscore the need for comprehensive **regulation** of AI in politics. Governments must act to protect the **integrity** of the democratic process by regulating the use of AI for political purposes, ensuring that it is not used to manipulate, deceive, or unfairly influence voters.

Summary

In this chapter, we explored the profound **impact of AI on democracy**, focusing on how AI can influence elections through social media algorithms, targeted ads, and the spread of misinformation. We discussed the need for **fair use of AI in politics**, highlighting the importance of transparency, accountability, and ethical considerations in political campaigns.

We examined the risks of **AI-driven political manipulation**, emphasizing the need for regulation to prevent AI from undermining democratic processes. The chapter also included a **real-world example** of the **Cambridge Analytica scandal**, which demonstrated how AI could be used unethically to manipulate voters, raising ethical concerns about privacy, transparency, and the role of data in elections.

As AI continues to play a larger role in political campaigns, it is essential to ensure that its use respects democratic principles, promotes fairness, and protects the integrity of elections. By creating strong ethical frameworks and regulatory guidelines, we can ensure that AI contributes positively to democratic processes rather than undermining them.

CHAPTER 23

Trust and Accountability in AI Systems

Building Trust in AI: The Importance of Trust in the Adoption of AI

For AI technologies to be widely accepted and effectively integrated into critical areas such as **healthcare, finance, criminal justice**, and **public services**, trust is paramount. Without trust, stakeholders—whether they are users, employees, or the general public—will hesitate to adopt or rely on AI systems. The foundation of trust in AI systems lies in their **reliability, predictability, fairness**, and **transparency**.

1. **Trust as a Key to Adoption**:
    o AI adoption is largely driven by the **perceived reliability** and **fairness** of the technology. For instance, in industries such as **healthcare**, where AI is being used for diagnostic tools and treatment recommendations, doctors must trust the system's outputs before relying on them for patient care. Likewise, in **finance**, customers need to trust that AI-powered tools are providing fair and unbiased recommendations regarding loans, insurance, or investments.
    o **Example**: In autonomous vehicles, public trust is crucial for widespread adoption. People need to trust that the system will

make safe and accurate decisions when driving in complex environments like busy urban streets. Any failure or accident that involves autonomous vehicles can significantly undermine public trust in AI technology.

2. **Key Factors for Building Trust**:
   o **Reliability**: AI systems must function consistently and produce accurate results. Unreliable AI systems erode trust and hinder adoption. For example, in **credit scoring** systems, inconsistencies or errors in scoring could result in unfair financial decisions that harm individuals.
   o **Transparency**: People are more likely to trust AI systems when they understand how decisions are made. Transparent algorithms that provide explanations for their decisions are key to building trust. **Explainability** ensures that individuals understand why AI systems make certain predictions or recommendations, increasing confidence in their use.
   o **Fairness and Bias Mitigation**: AI systems must be fair and free from discrimination. When AI systems are perceived as biased or discriminatory, such as in **hiring algorithms** or **criminal justice sentencing tools**, trust is lost, and stakeholders may seek alternatives.

3. **Ethical and Social Responsibility**:
   o Building trust also involves the social responsibility of AI developers to

consider the ethical implications of their systems. AI systems should be designed with the public good in mind, ensuring that their deployment does not cause harm to individuals or communities.

o **Example**: In **healthcare**, trust is built when AI systems are developed with patient privacy and confidentiality in mind. Ensuring **data protection** through methods like encryption and anonymization helps secure sensitive personal health information and build trust in the system.

Ensuring Accountability: Establishing Clear Lines of Responsibility for AI Decisions

As AI systems make decisions that affect individuals' lives, **accountability** becomes a critical concern. Clear lines of responsibility must be established to ensure that someone is held accountable when things go wrong. This is especially important in sectors like **criminal justice**, **healthcare**, and **finance**, where the stakes are high, and mistakes can have significant consequences.

1. **Accountability in Decision-Making**:
   o **AI Decision-Making**: AI systems often make complex decisions that can impact people's lives, such as determining whether a loan is approved, predicting the likelihood of a crime, or diagnosing a medical condition. For AI systems to be

trusted, the decision-making process must be **traceable** and **justifiable**.

- o **Responsibility for AI Decisions**: When an AI system makes a decision that negatively affects an individual (e.g., wrongfully denying a loan, wrongly diagnosing a health condition, or sentencing a person to jail), it must be clear who is responsible for that decision. This includes **AI developers**, **companies**, and **governments** that deploy the system.
- o **Example**: In the case of an AI-powered criminal justice tool like **COMPAS** (a risk assessment tool used to predict the likelihood of reoffending), if the system incorrectly predicts that an individual is high-risk when they are not, there needs to be clear accountability for how this mistake occurred and who is responsible for correcting it.

2. **Establishing Accountability Mechanisms**:
- o **Human Oversight**: While AI can make decisions autonomously, human oversight is essential to ensure accountability. Humans should be involved in critical decision-making processes, particularly in high-stakes areas. This includes ensuring that there is an option for individuals to **appeal** decisions made by AI systems and for these appeals to be reviewed by a human operator.

- o **Audit Trails and Documentation**: AI systems should maintain **audit trails** that document their decision-making process, enabling stakeholders to trace how a decision was made. This transparency helps ensure accountability, especially in instances where the decision leads to harm.
- o **Legal and Ethical Frameworks**: Clear **legal** and **ethical** frameworks should be established to determine the limits of AI decision-making and to ensure that humans are held responsible for AI decisions when necessary.
- o **Example**: In **autonomous vehicles**, if the AI system makes a decision that leads to an accident, human drivers, manufacturers, or developers must be held accountable. Laws and regulations should provide clear guidelines on liability in such situations.

3. **Ensuring Organizational Accountability**:
- o **Corporate Responsibility**: Companies that develop and deploy AI systems should be responsible for the outcomes of these systems. This includes ensuring that AI models are regularly tested for **bias** and **fairness** and that appropriate measures are in place to prevent harmful outcomes.
- o **Example**: **Amazon**'s use of AI in warehouse management has faced criticism due to its impact on workers.

The company must be held accountable for ensuring that AI systems are not overly restrictive or harmful to employee well-being.

Creating Transparent AI Systems: Practices for Making AI Accountable to Stakeholders

Transparency and **accountability** go hand in hand in the development of ethical AI systems. For AI systems to be truly accountable to stakeholders, transparency must be woven into every phase of the development process—from the design and deployment stages to the ongoing monitoring and evaluation of the system.

1. **Clear Documentation and Communication**:
   o **Explaining AI Decisions**: AI models, especially **complex models** such as deep learning systems, should be designed to explain their reasoning in clear, understandable terms. This means that both the developers and the end-users should be able to explain why a particular decision was made by the AI system. Making complex models more interpretable is key to ensuring transparency.
   o **Documentation**: Comprehensive documentation should be created to explain how AI models were trained, the datasets used, the assumptions made, and the decision-making processes of the AI system. This documentation should be

publicly available for scrutiny, particularly in high-stakes sectors like healthcare and criminal justice.

- o **Example**: For an AI-powered healthcare system that recommends treatment plans, developers should document how the system was trained, what data was used, and how the algorithm determines the best course of action.

2. **Transparency in Data Usage**:
   - o **Data Collection and Usage**: AI systems rely heavily on data. Transparency about how data is collected, processed, and used is crucial for ensuring that individuals' **privacy** is respected and that data usage complies with **ethical guidelines** and **privacy laws**.
   - o **Example**: A financial institution using AI to assess creditworthiness should clearly communicate to customers how their personal data is being used in the decision-making process, and customers should have the option to consent to this data usage.

3. **Engaging Stakeholders**:
   - o AI developers must engage with **stakeholders**—including affected individuals, regulatory bodies, and independent auditors—throughout the development and deployment process. Engaging with stakeholders helps identify potential risks and ensures that the system

is transparent and accountable to those who will be affected by it.

- o **Example**: In the case of **AI-driven hiring tools**, employers should involve employees, applicants, and labor rights organizations to ensure that the system is fair and transparent. Stakeholders can provide valuable input on potential biases and areas where the AI system could be improved.

4. **Ongoing Monitoring and Feedback**:
   - o Transparency is not a one-time event; it requires continuous **monitoring** and **feedback** to ensure that the system continues to function as intended. Regular audits, user feedback, and independent assessments can help maintain transparency and accountability, ensuring that the AI system does not evolve in ways that undermine trust or fairness.
   - o **Example**: An AI system used in **criminal justice** for sentencing recommendations should be continuously audited and updated based on real-world feedback to ensure that it does not inadvertently perpetuate biases in the justice system.

Real-World Example: AI Accountability in Criminal Justice Sentencing

AI tools are increasingly used in the criminal justice system to assist with decisions such as **sentencing**, **parole**, and **risk assessment**. While these tools aim to increase efficiency and objectivity, they raise concerns about accountability, transparency, and fairness.

1. **COMPAS and Risk Assessment**:
   - **COMPAS (Correctional Offender Management Profiling for Alternative Sanctions)** is a risk assessment tool used in the U.S. criminal justice system to assess the likelihood of a defendant reoffending. However, the system has been criticized for potentially being biased against African American defendants, who may be unfairly classified as high-risk based on historical data that reflects societal biases.
   - **Accountability Issues**: When COMPAS makes a prediction about the likelihood of reoffending, the decision is not always transparent, and individuals are often unable to challenge or understand the reasoning behind the assessment. This raises accountability concerns, especially when the outcomes significantly impact a person's life, such as in sentencing or parole decisions.
2. **Transparency and Bias Concerns**:
   - Despite the use of AI systems like COMPAS, it remains unclear how exactly the tool arrives at its decisions, and the data used to train the model has been shown to reflect systemic biases. This lack of transparency and accountability

leads to questions about the fairness of the system.

- o **Efforts for Accountability**: In response to these concerns, advocates have called for greater transparency in AI models used in criminal justice, including making the underlying algorithms and data used in risk assessment tools publicly available for scrutiny and providing defendants with the right to challenge AI-based decisions.

Summary

In this chapter, we examined the importance of **trust** and **accountability** in AI systems. Trust is essential for the adoption and effective use of AI technologies, particularly in high-stakes areas such as **healthcare**, **criminal justice**, and **finance**. We discussed how transparency in AI decision-making, clear lines of accountability, and ethical practices can help build trust in AI systems.

We also explored how to **create transparent AI systems** through comprehensive documentation, data usage transparency, and stakeholder engagement. By ensuring that AI systems are understandable, accountable, and continuously monitored, we can foster greater trust and accountability.

The chapter included a **real-world example** of AI accountability in the **criminal justice system**. We examined how AI systems like COMPAS have raised ethical concerns about bias, transparency, and fairness, underscoring the need for clear accountability mechanisms in AI systems that impact individuals' lives.

As AI continues to be integrated into critical sectors, it is crucial to ensure that these systems are developed and deployed with integrity, transparency, and a clear framework of accountability, ensuring that AI serves society in a responsible and trustworthy manner.

CHAPTER 24

The Evolution of Ethical AI Design

Historical Context of AI Ethics: From Early AI Research to Modern Concerns

The field of **artificial intelligence** (AI) has undergone significant transformations since its inception in the mid-20th century. Alongside technical advancements, the ethical implications of AI technologies have evolved, reflecting both the growing capabilities of AI systems and the increasing awareness of their societal impact.

1. **Early AI Research and Ethics**:
   o The origins of AI can be traced back to the **1940s** and **1950s**, with the works of pioneers like **Alan Turing**, who proposed the famous **Turing Test** as a way to evaluate a machine's ability to exhibit intelligent behavior. Early AI research focused on theoretical frameworks and simple problem-solving systems, but ethical considerations were largely overlooked in these initial stages.
   o **Turing's Ethical Vision**: While Turing didn't directly address the ethics of AI in his work, his question "Can machines think?" laid the foundation for later debates about the role of AI in society. Early on, the ethical implications of AI were speculative at best, with much of the

244

focus on whether machines could ever exhibit true intelligence or consciousness.

2. **The Rise of Expert Systems and the Ethical Concerns of the 1970s-1990s**:
   - In the **1970s** and **1980s**, AI research progressed with the development of **expert systems**, which were designed to mimic human expertise in specific domains like medicine and finance. However, these systems raised ethical questions about **decision-making** and **accountability**. For instance, should an AI system be responsible for making life-altering decisions, like diagnosing diseases or recommending legal sentences?
   - The emergence of AI technologies that could influence critical areas of human life brought the first serious discussions about **ethical guidelines** in AI design. These concerns largely centered around **data privacy**, **transparency**, and the potential for AI to perpetuate biases.

3. **AI Ethics in the 21st Century**:
   - In the 2000s and 2010s, the rapid growth of AI capabilities—fueled by **machine learning, deep learning**, and **big data**—brought AI into mainstream applications. The increased reliance on AI in high-stakes domains such as **healthcare, autonomous vehicles**, and **criminal justice** intensified concerns over **bias, privacy violations**, and **human rights**.

o The introduction of **autonomous systems** (like self-driving cars) and **AI in decision-making** (like predictive policing or hiring algorithms) has raised critical ethical questions. Today, the focus has shifted towards **accountability** (who is responsible when AI makes mistakes?), **fairness** (how to avoid biased decisions?), and **transparency** (how to explain AI decisions to the public?).

The Evolution of Ethical Standards: How AI Ethics Have Developed Over Time

As AI technologies have advanced, so too have the ethical frameworks that guide their development and deployment. Ethical AI design has evolved from basic concerns about privacy and safety to a more nuanced focus on **human rights**, **social justice**, and **accountability**.

1. **Early Ethical Frameworks**:
   o Early ethical concerns in AI were largely driven by philosophers, scientists, and ethicists who speculated about the implications of machine intelligence. **Isaac Asimov's Three Laws of Robotics**, proposed in his science fiction works, introduced the idea of ethical guidelines for AI behavior. These laws were fictional but illustrated an early attempt to address the consequences of autonomous machines.

- As AI technology began to influence practical applications, more formal ethical frameworks emerged, but they were primarily focused on privacy concerns and **algorithmic transparency**.

2. **The Rise of Ethical Guidelines and Regulations (2000s - Present)**:
    - In the **2000s**, as AI started impacting more aspects of daily life, discussions about **AI ethics** became more formalized. Various organizations, including the **IEEE, OECD**, and **EU**, began working on ethical guidelines for AI development. The **OECD Principles on Artificial Intelligence** (2019) were among the first internationally recognized ethical standards, emphasizing the need for AI systems to be **fair**, **transparent**, and **accountable**.
    - In the **2010s**, the discussion around AI ethics expanded to include issues like **algorithmic bias**, **discrimination**, and the responsibility of AI creators. Regulatory bodies, such as the **European Union**, began drafting more comprehensive **AI regulations**, culminating in the **EU AI Act**, which outlines clear rules for high-risk AI systems and emphasizes ethical considerations.

3. **Ethical AI as a Core Principle (2020s)**:
    - By the **2020s**, ethical AI has become a core principle in the AI industry. Leading

companies and organizations now integrate ethical considerations into every stage of AI development, from research and design to deployment and post-deployment evaluation.

- **Diversity, equity, and inclusion** have become central pillars of ethical AI design, with a focus on ensuring that AI systems are developed with fairness and accessibility in mind. The importance of **human oversight** and ensuring **accountability** for AI decisions has been increasingly recognized as essential for preventing harm.
- **Example**: The AI ethics frameworks proposed by **Google**, **Microsoft**, and **IBM** reflect this shift, with each company emphasizing the need for **ethical accountability** and promoting diversity in AI training data to avoid biased outcomes.

The Future of Ethical AI Design: Emerging Trends and Innovations in Ethical AI

As AI continues to advance, new ethical challenges will arise, and existing frameworks will need to adapt. Here are some emerging trends and innovations that are likely to shape the future of ethical AI design.

1. **AI for Social Good**:
   - A growing trend in AI development is the emphasis on using AI for **social good**. AI

technologies are being developed and applied to address global challenges such as **climate change**, **global health**, **poverty**, and **education**. In the future, AI systems will increasingly be used to solve societal problems, while ensuring that ethical considerations are incorporated into their design and deployment.

- o **Example**: AI applications in **predictive healthcare** are being developed to identify disease outbreaks, assist in diagnosis, and optimize resource allocation in low-resource settings. These innovations aim to improve health outcomes while adhering to strict ethical standards of fairness and data privacy.

2. **AI and Human Rights**:
    - o **Human rights** will continue to play a central role in AI ethics, particularly in terms of **privacy, freedom of expression**, and **non-discrimination**. As AI systems become more embedded in our daily lives, ensuring that they uphold **fundamental rights** will be critical.
    - o **Example**: As AI technologies are increasingly used in **border control, immigration**, and **surveillance**, there will be increased focus on ensuring that these systems do not violate individuals' privacy or freedom of movement.

3. **Explainable and Interpretable AI**:
    - o One of the most important areas of innovation in ethical AI is the

development of **explainable AI** (XAI) systems. The need for AI systems to explain their decisions in human-understandable terms is essential for building trust and ensuring accountability. Researchers are developing methods to make even the most complex AI models more interpretable, addressing one of the biggest concerns in AI ethics.

○ **Example**: In **autonomous vehicles**, AI models will need to provide real-time explanations for decisions made during critical moments (e.g., in accident-avoidance situations), ensuring that those decisions can be understood and evaluated by human operators.

4. **AI in Autonomous Systems**:
   ○ The development of **autonomous AI systems**, such as self-driving cars and drones, presents complex ethical challenges, especially regarding accountability in case of accidents or unintended harm. The future of ethical AI will likely involve new frameworks for regulating autonomous systems, ensuring they operate safely, fairly, and responsibly.
   ○ **Example**: **Autonomous drones** used in military or surveillance applications raise ethical concerns about privacy, surveillance, and the potential for misuse. As these technologies evolve, strong

ethical frameworks will be required to ensure they align with international human rights laws.

5. **AI Governance and Global Cooperation**:
   o The future of ethical AI will require continued **global cooperation** to create universal guidelines and standards. As AI technologies evolve, international **regulatory bodies** and frameworks will play a key role in ensuring that AI is developed and used ethically across the globe. Efforts to **regulate AI ethics** globally will help prevent misuse, ensure fairness, and protect vulnerable populations from harm.
   o **Example**: The **OECD** and the **United Nations** are already working together to create international agreements and frameworks for ethical AI, setting the stage for a more cooperative approach to regulating AI technologies worldwide.

Real-World Example: The Changing Ethics of AI in Military Applications

One of the most significant areas where AI ethics are evolving is in the domain of **military applications**. AI is increasingly being used to develop autonomous weapons systems, surveillance drones, and **predictive tools** for military decision-making. While these technologies hold the potential for improving security and defense capabilities, they also raise profound ethical concerns.

1. **Autonomous Weapons Systems (AWS)**:
   o **Autonomous weapons systems** use AI to identify and engage targets without human intervention. While these systems can enhance military capabilities, they also raise concerns about **accountability** (who is responsible if an autonomous weapon makes a mistake?), **human oversight** (should humans always be in control of life-and-death decisions?), and **international laws** (how should AWS be regulated under international law?).
   o **Ethical Debate**: The use of AI in autonomous weapons systems raises ethical questions about the potential for machines to make life-or-death decisions. Many ethicists argue that humans should always retain control over lethal force, while others believe that AI can be trusted to act more objectively than humans in high-pressure situations.
2. **AI for Surveillance and Targeting**:
   o AI-driven surveillance systems, such as drones and satellite imaging, are being used to track movements, identify potential threats, and target specific individuals. While these technologies can enhance security, they also raise concerns about **privacy violations**, **civil liberties**, and the potential for **unintended harm** to civilians.
   o **Example**: The use of AI-powered drones for targeted strikes in military operations

has raised concerns about the **accuracy** of targeting, the **risk of civilian casualties**, and the ethical implications of **preemptive strikes** based on AI predictions.

3. **Regulation of AI in Military Applications**:
   - As AI becomes more prevalent in military settings, international efforts will be required to establish **ethical guidelines** and **regulations** to govern its use. There is growing support for a **global ban** on fully autonomous weapons systems, and efforts are underway to develop international agreements that regulate the use of AI in military operations.
   - **Example**: The **Campaign to Stop Killer Robots**, a global movement calling for a ban on autonomous weapons, argues that AI-driven weapons could lower the threshold for war and lead to unintended escalation and harm.

Summary

In this chapter, we explored the **evolution of ethical AI design**, starting from early concerns in AI research to the modern ethical issues that have emerged as AI systems become integral to society. We discussed how AI ethics have developed over time, from basic concerns about privacy to more nuanced issues involving **bias**, **accountability**, and **human rights**.

Looking to the future, we highlighted **emerging trends** and innovations in ethical AI, including the use of AI for **social good**, the development of **explainable AI**, and the need for global **cooperation** on AI regulation. We also examined a **real-world example** of the changing ethics of AI in **military applications**, where the development of **autonomous weapons** and AI-driven **surveillance systems** has raised profound ethical questions about **accountability**, **privacy**, and the potential for harm.

As AI technologies continue to evolve, it is critical that ethical considerations remain at the forefront of their development. The future of AI depends on creating systems that are not only technically advanced but also ethically sound, ensuring that these technologies serve the public good while safeguarding **human dignity** and **rights**.

CHAPTER 25

AI Ethics in Education

The Role of AI in Education: From Personalized Learning to Administrative Tools

AI has the potential to revolutionize **education** by enhancing both the learning experience for students and the efficiency of administrative tasks. With the integration of AI in educational systems, we can expect personalized, adaptive learning environments and streamlined administrative processes that save time and resources. However, this also raises important ethical questions about fairness, privacy, and accessibility.

1. **Personalized Learning**:
   - One of the most promising applications of AI in education is **personalized learning**. AI can analyze data about students' strengths, weaknesses, learning styles, and progress, allowing for the creation of **adaptive learning systems** that tailor content and teaching methods to each student's unique needs. This helps students progress at their own pace and ensures they receive targeted support where needed.
   - **Example**: **AI-powered platforms** like **DreamBox** and **Knewton** provide personalized learning experiences, adjusting the difficulty of questions or

offering additional resources based on a student's performance.

2. **Intelligent Tutoring Systems**:
   - o **AI tutoring systems** can help students learn by providing immediate feedback, offering explanations, and guiding them through problems step-by-step. These systems can act as supplementary resources to human teachers, enabling individualized attention for students even when teachers are unavailable.
   - o **Example**: Systems like **Carnegie Learning's MATHia** provide AI-driven tutoring in mathematics, offering personalized guidance and real-time support tailored to the learner's needs.

3. **Administrative Tools**:
   - o AI is also being used to streamline administrative functions in educational institutions, from grading and attendance tracking to curriculum design and resource management. By automating routine tasks, AI frees up time for educators to focus on teaching and student engagement.
   - o **Example**: AI-driven systems can help automate **grading** by analyzing student submissions and providing consistent, objective feedback, particularly in subjects like **multiple-choice tests**, **essays**, and **coding assignments**.

4. **AI-Enhanced Student Support**:

- o AI tools are increasingly being used to offer **student support services**, such as chatbots and virtual assistants that answer questions about schedules, assignments, and deadlines. These systems help students navigate the complexities of academic life and provide instant access to essential information.
- o **Example**: Chatbots like **Georgia Tech's Jill Watson** assist students with routine questions and administrative tasks, providing 24/7 support and reducing the workload of teaching assistants.

Ethical Considerations in AI-Driven Education: Fairness, Data Privacy, and Access

While AI in education holds immense promise, there are critical **ethical considerations** that must be addressed to ensure that these technologies benefit all students and do not perpetuate inequalities.

1. **Fairness**:
   - o **Bias in AI systems** is a major concern in education. AI systems, especially those used for personalized learning or grading, can unintentionally reinforce **pre-existing biases** if they are trained on biased datasets. This can lead to unfair outcomes, such as certain groups of students receiving less support or facing lower expectations based on their race,

socioeconomic background, or other demographic factors.

- o **Example**: If an AI system used for **personalized learning** is trained predominantly on data from students in **wealthier schools**, it may not be able to cater effectively to students from lower-income backgrounds, resulting in **inequitable learning experiences**.

2. **Data Privacy**:
   - o AI systems in education often rely on vast amounts of personal data, including student performance, behavior, and even biometric data. This raises important questions about **data privacy** and **student consent**. How should students' data be collected, stored, and used? Who owns the data, and who is responsible for protecting it?
   - o **Example**: AI-powered learning platforms collect data on students' activities, but there are concerns about how this data might be shared with third parties or used for purposes beyond education, such as targeted marketing or surveillance.

3. **Access and Inequality**:
   - o One of the greatest risks of AI in education is the potential to exacerbate existing **inequities**. Students in **underfunded schools** may not have access to the same AI-driven resources as those in more affluent areas, leading to a digital divide. Moreover, **AI tools** may

not always account for the diverse needs of students with disabilities or those who speak different languages.

- o **Example**: Students in rural or low-income areas may not have access to the **internet** or devices needed to use AI-powered educational platforms, putting them at a disadvantage compared to their urban peers who have better access to technology.

4. **The Risk of Over-Dependence on AI**:
   - o While AI can be an excellent tool for enhancing education, there is a risk that students and educators may become overly reliant on technology, reducing the importance of human interaction and critical thinking in the learning process.
   - o **Example**: Over-reliance on AI tutors for subjects like math could lead to **students missing out on the collaborative, problem-solving skills** they gain from interacting with teachers and peers.

Designing Ethical Educational AI Systems: Ensuring That AI in Education Benefits All Students

To ensure that AI systems in education benefit all students and do not perpetuate inequalities, designers and policymakers must prioritize **ethical AI development**. This involves creating AI systems that are **fair**, **transparent**, and **accessible** for all students, regardless of their background, location, or abilities.

1. **Bias Mitigation**:
   - Developers of AI-driven educational tools must actively work to **mitigate bias** by ensuring that training datasets are diverse and representative of different student populations. This includes collecting data from a wide range of educational settings, demographics, and cultural contexts to avoid reinforcing existing inequalities.
   - **Example**: To avoid bias, AI learning platforms should use **diverse datasets** and undergo regular **audits** to ensure that the system does not favor one group of students over another. This might involve ensuring that the AI provides equal opportunities for students of different races, genders, socioeconomic statuses, and abilities.
2. **Inclusive Design**:
   - AI systems in education should be designed to meet the needs of **all learners**, including those with disabilities, non-native speakers, and students with different learning styles. This requires making the systems adaptable and **inclusive**, offering support features like **speech-to-text**, **captioning**, or **language translation**.
   - **Example**: AI-driven tutoring systems should be able to adjust to the needs of students with learning disabilities, such as those with **dyslexia**, by offering

customized learning experiences that include **audio-based** or **visual aids**.

3. **Data Privacy and Consent**:
   - **Data privacy** should be a priority in the design of educational AI systems. Students and their parents (where applicable) should be informed about what data is being collected, how it will be used, and who will have access to it. AI systems must be designed with strict data protection measures in place to safeguard students' privacy.
   - **Example**: AI-powered education platforms should follow **GDPR** guidelines or similar data privacy laws to ensure that students' data is only used for educational purposes and that it is kept secure.

4. **Transparency and Accountability**:
   - **Transparency** is crucial for ensuring that stakeholders—students, parents, and educators—understand how AI systems work and make decisions. This includes providing clear explanations of how AI systems assess student progress, make recommendations, or grade assignments. Developers must also establish mechanisms for **accountability** when AI systems make errors or fail to deliver equitable outcomes.
   - **Example**: In AI-driven **grading systems**, students should be able to receive explanations for how their grades were

calculated and have an opportunity to appeal any decisions made by the system.

5. **Collaboration with Educators**:
    o To create ethical AI systems, developers should work closely with **educators** to ensure that the technology aligns with educational goals. Teachers and administrators are essential partners in designing systems that support, rather than replace, human instruction.
    o **Example**: Teachers should be involved in the design and implementation of AI tutoring systems to ensure that these systems complement traditional teaching methods and address students' learning needs effectively.

Real-World Example: AI-Powered Tutoring Systems and the Risks of Bias

AI-powered tutoring systems, such as those used in **mathematics**, **language learning**, and **science**, are becoming increasingly popular as personalized educational tools. While these systems can provide students with immediate feedback and customized learning paths, they also pose risks related to **bias** and **inequality**.

1. **AI Tutoring in Math**:
    o Platforms like **Socratic** and **Khan Academy's** AI-powered learning tools use algorithms to provide personalized learning experiences in subjects like

math. However, if the training data used to build these systems is not representative, the AI can unintentionally favor certain types of learners over others.

- o **Risk of Bias**: For example, if the AI is trained primarily on data from students in affluent urban schools, it might not adapt well to students from rural or underfunded schools, where learning conditions may differ significantly.
- o **Example**: An AI tutor might give more opportunities for **advanced problem-solving** to students from well-resourced schools, while students from less-resourced schools might struggle due to the system's bias toward more advanced learners.

2. **Addressing Bias in AI Tutoring**:
    - o Developers must take steps to ensure that AI tutoring systems are inclusive and provide equitable opportunities for all students. This involves using **diverse datasets**, offering **adjustable learning paths**, and incorporating feedback from **teachers** and **students**.
    - o **Example**: Companies that build AI-powered tutors should perform regular **bias audits** and include **feedback mechanisms** for students to report discrepancies or biases in the system's performance.

Summary

In this chapter, we explored the role of **AI in education** and discussed the ethical challenges it presents, including issues of **fairness**, **data privacy**, and **access**. We examined how AI can transform education through **personalized learning**, **intelligent tutoring systems**, and **administrative tools** but also highlighted the risks of bias, inequity, and over-reliance on technology.

We discussed how to **design ethical educational AI systems** by addressing issues of **bias**, **inclusivity**, **data privacy**, and **accountability**. Ensuring that AI systems are developed in collaboration with **educators** and are **transparent** and **fair** is essential for maximizing the benefits of AI while minimizing harm.

The chapter also provided a **real-world example** of **AI-powered tutoring systems**, focusing on the risks of bias and the importance of making these systems equitable for all students. To create AI systems that truly benefit education, developers must prioritize ethical considerations, ensuring that AI serves all students fairly and supports their learning in meaningful ways.

CHAPTER 26

Building Ethical AI Teams

The Importance of Diverse AI Teams: Promoting Diversity for Better Decision-Making

Diversity in AI teams is not just a **moral** or **ethical** necessity—it is a **strategic advantage** that can improve the quality of AI systems and ensure that these systems reflect a broad range of perspectives. Diverse AI teams are better equipped to identify biases, understand different user needs, and make ethical decisions that benefit everyone. By integrating people from diverse backgrounds, AI teams can build more equitable, inclusive, and robust systems.

1. **Diversity and Bias Reduction**:
    o AI models are only as good as the data used to train them and the people who build them. If AI development teams lack diversity, they may unintentionally embed their own biases into the models they create. For example, if a team is homogenous—whether in terms of race, gender, or socioeconomic background—it may not be attuned to the challenges faced by underrepresented groups, leading to **biased algorithms**.
    o **Example**: In the past, facial recognition algorithms have been shown to perform poorly for people of color, particularly women. This issue could have been

265

mitigated if more diverse voices were involved in the development process, particularly those who could identify the problem early on.

2. **Improved Decision-Making**:
   o **Diverse teams** bring different experiences and perspectives, leading to more comprehensive decision-making. AI systems often involve complex, high-stakes decisions that impact individuals and communities. When teams lack diversity, they may miss critical insights or fail to account for the full spectrum of users affected by the technology.
   o **Example**: In the case of a hiring algorithm, a diverse team is more likely to recognize when the model's training data inadvertently discriminates against certain groups, such as women or minority candidates, and take corrective action to address those biases.

3. **Broader Reach of AI Systems**:
   o AI technologies are used globally, affecting people from different cultures, languages, and backgrounds. Diverse teams bring a more holistic understanding of how AI systems can affect different communities and can work toward designing systems that serve a broader audience. This results in AI products that are more **inclusive** and **global** in scope.
   o **Example**: AI-driven healthcare systems designed by diverse teams are more likely

to account for various cultural contexts and health disparities, ensuring that the systems serve the needs of a global population, rather than only a specific demographic.

Creating Ethical AI Cultures: Building Organizations That Prioritize Responsible AI

Creating an **ethical AI culture** requires more than just assembling a diverse team; it requires embedding ethical principles into the organizational framework. This involves establishing clear values, promoting transparency, and ensuring that AI systems are developed with **responsibility** and **accountability** at the forefront.

1. **Establishing Ethical Standards**:
    o   Ethical principles must be ingrained in the organization's mission, vision, and values. Organizations should establish formal ethical guidelines and standards that govern the development and deployment of AI systems. These standards should prioritize **human rights**, **fairness**, **transparency**, and **accountability** at every stage of the AI lifecycle.
    o   **Example**: Companies like **Google** and **Microsoft** have created **AI ethics boards** that provide oversight and ensure that their AI initiatives align with ethical guidelines. These boards are responsible

for reviewing new AI projects and ensuring that they adhere to the company's values regarding privacy, fairness, and non-discrimination.

2. **Embedding Ethics in the Development Process**:
   - Ethical considerations should be integrated at every stage of the AI development process. This means that AI ethics must be considered during **design**, **data collection**, **training**, and **deployment**. Developers should be encouraged to think about the ethical implications of their work and assess potential risks before AI systems are launched.
   - **Example**: **IBM** has integrated **ethical checkpoints** in its AI development process, where developers must evaluate the potential biases, fairness, and ethical risks of their AI models before they are deployed. This ensures that AI systems are evaluated for ethical concerns throughout the development lifecycle.

3. **Transparency and Accountability**:
   - A strong ethical culture requires transparency in decision-making and accountability for the outcomes of AI systems. Organizations should be open about how their AI systems are designed, how they make decisions, and what data they rely on. Moreover, they should be accountable for the impact of their AI

technologies on individuals and society, ensuring that ethical concerns are addressed when problems arise.

- o **Example**: **OpenAI**, the company behind GPT-3, has prioritized transparency in its research and development processes. It releases detailed research papers, guidelines, and safety measures, and it engages with the broader AI community to ensure that its technologies are used ethically.

4. **Promoting Ethical Leadership**:
- o Leadership plays a critical role in shaping the organizational culture and driving ethical practices. AI leaders should set an example by championing ethical AI, allocating resources to promote ethics education, and encouraging open discussions about the moral implications of AI systems.
- o **Example**: **Satya Nadella**, CEO of Microsoft, has been a strong advocate for **responsible AI**. He has emphasized the need for AI to be developed with ethical considerations and has supported the creation of **ethical AI frameworks** within the company.

Training and Educating AI Developers on Ethics: Preparing the Next Generation of AI Professionals

As AI becomes more embedded in society, it is essential that the next generation of AI professionals is equipped with the knowledge and tools to create ethical AI systems. **AI education and training** should include not only technical skills but also a strong understanding of the ethical challenges and responsibilities associated with AI development.

1. **Integrating Ethics into AI Curriculum**:
   - **Ethics education** should be a core component of AI curricula in universities and technical institutions. AI developers must learn about the social, legal, and ethical implications of their work, as well as the tools and frameworks available to address issues like **bias**, **privacy**, and **accountability**.
   - **Example**: Universities like **Stanford** and **MIT** offer specialized courses on **AI ethics**, where students learn about topics such as **machine fairness**, **algorithmic bias**, and **AI governance**. These courses help prepare future AI developers to think critically about the ethical implications of their work.
2. **Workshops and Ongoing Education**:
   - For professionals already working in AI development, companies should offer **workshops**, **seminars**, and **ongoing training** on ethical AI practices. Regular training ensures that AI developers stay updated on the latest ethical guidelines and learn how to apply them to their projects.

- o **Example**: **Google** offers an **AI ethics training program** for its engineers, focusing on the responsible design and deployment of AI systems. The program covers topics such as **algorithmic fairness**, **privacy protection**, and **AI accountability**.

3. **Cross-Disciplinary Collaboration**:
   - o AI developers should be encouraged to collaborate with experts from other fields, such as **law**, **sociology**, **psychology**, and **philosophy**. This cross-disciplinary approach allows developers to better understand the broader impact of AI systems and make more informed decisions about their design and deployment.
   - o **Example**: In the development of AI systems for healthcare, collaboration with medical professionals, ethicists, and patient advocates ensures that the technology aligns with **ethical standards** and meets the diverse needs of patients.

Real-World Example: Diversity Initiatives in AI Development Teams at Large Tech Companies

The importance of **diversity** in AI development teams has become a key focus for many of the largest tech companies, especially as AI has begun to play a larger role in decision-making across society. Major tech firms have launched **diversity initiatives** aimed at creating more inclusive AI teams that are better equipped to design fair and ethical AI systems.

1. **Google's AI Principles and Diversity Initiatives**:
   o Google has been a leader in AI ethics and diversity, publishing its **AI Principles** to ensure that AI is developed with fairness and transparency in mind. In addition to these principles, Google has committed to increasing diversity within its AI teams. The company has actively recruited more women, people of color, and individuals from underrepresented backgrounds in the tech industry to ensure that its AI products are developed with a broader perspective.
   o **Example**: Google's **AI for Social Good** initiative includes a focus on **diverse teams** to develop AI solutions for global challenges. By prioritizing diversity in AI teams, Google ensures that its technologies reflect a wide range of viewpoints and are designed to benefit a diverse global population.

2. **Microsoft's Commitment to Diversity in AI**:
   o Microsoft has also made significant strides in promoting diversity within its AI teams. The company has set goals for increasing the representation of **women** and **minorities** in its workforce, particularly in leadership and technical roles. By fostering an inclusive work

environment, Microsoft is able to create AI systems that are more attuned to the needs of diverse populations.

- o **Example**: Microsoft's **AI and Research** division has introduced several programs to support diversity, such as partnerships with organizations that encourage women and minorities to pursue careers in AI. This helps ensure that the company's AI products and services are developed with a broad understanding of the needs of various demographic groups.

3. **IBM's AI Ethics and Diversity in Development**:
   - o IBM has been a pioneer in creating responsible AI systems, integrating **ethical AI guidelines** and **diversity** efforts into its AI development process. The company has created programs to support the inclusion of diverse voices in the development of its AI technologies, particularly by focusing on ensuring that AI systems are free from bias and are built with input from diverse communities.
   - o **Example**: IBM has launched a series of **AI ethics workshops** and diversity initiatives, aiming to create AI systems that reflect the values of inclusivity and fairness. The company's focus on **diverse teams** ensures that its AI systems are more likely to address a wide range of societal challenges and avoid perpetuating existing biases.

Summary

In this chapter, we explored the importance of **building ethical AI teams** and the key practices required to ensure that AI development prioritizes responsibility and fairness. **Diversity** in AI teams plays a crucial role in improving decision-making, reducing bias, and ensuring that AI technologies are inclusive and equitable. **Creating ethical AI cultures** within organizations, offering **training on AI ethics**, and fostering **cross-disciplinary collaboration** are essential steps toward achieving ethical AI outcomes.

We also examined **real-world examples** of diversity initiatives in AI development teams at major tech companies like **Google**, **Microsoft**, and **IBM**, demonstrating how these organizations are working to ensure that AI systems are developed with diverse perspectives and ethical considerations in mind.

As AI continues to shape our world, building ethical AI teams that reflect diverse voices and prioritize fairness will be essential for ensuring that AI technologies benefit all people and serve the public good.

CHAPTER 27

The Future of Ethical AI Design

What's Next for Ethical AI?: Emerging Challenges and Future Directions in AI Ethics

As AI technology continues to evolve and become deeply integrated into various aspects of society, the ethical challenges surrounding its use are becoming more complex. The future of ethical AI design will be shaped by **new advancements** in AI capabilities, **emerging ethical concerns**, and the ongoing need to ensure that AI systems benefit society while minimizing harm.

1. **The Growing Complexity of AI Systems**:
    o AI systems are becoming more **complex** and **autonomous**, with deep learning models and neural networks that are difficult to interpret or explain. As AI evolves, it will be increasingly important to create systems that are not only effective but also understandable and **accountable**. The challenge of maintaining transparency and ensuring that these systems make decisions in ways that are fair, ethical, and explainable will continue to grow.
    o **Example**: As AI systems become more **self-learning** and capable of evolving their own decision-making strategies, the need for regulatory frameworks and

ethical guidelines will become even more urgent to prevent unintended consequences or the perpetuation of harmful biases.

2. **Bias and Fairness in the Age of Big Data**:
    o The use of massive datasets to train AI models has the potential to introduce new forms of **bias** that can have far-reaching implications. As AI models learn from data generated by society, they can inadvertently reinforce existing inequalities in areas like hiring, criminal justice, and healthcare. In the future, addressing issues of fairness and bias in AI will require more sophisticated techniques for detecting, mitigating, and preventing these biases.
    o **Example**: **Facial recognition** technology, when trained on biased data, may fail to recognize people from diverse racial backgrounds accurately. Ensuring fairness in AI will require developing better methods to diversify the data used for training models and create algorithms that are robust and unbiased.

3. **Ethics in Autonomous Systems**:
    o **Autonomous systems**, such as self-driving cars and drones, present unique ethical dilemmas that will continue to evolve. These systems must be able to make decisions that balance safety, efficiency, and fairness, often in high-stakes environments. As these systems

gain more responsibility, the ethical questions around accountability, decision-making, and risk management will become more pronounced.

- o **Example**: In the context of **autonomous vehicles**, ethical decisions need to be made about how these systems respond in critical situations (e.g., if an accident is unavoidable). Should an AI prioritize saving the driver, passengers, or pedestrians? Developing ethical frameworks to guide such decisions will be a major challenge for the future of AI.

4. **Global AI Governance**:

- o As AI technologies continue to impact global society, international cooperation will be essential to address **global AI ethics**. Currently, there is no universal framework for AI governance, and different countries have different approaches to regulating AI. In the future, establishing **global standards** for AI will be critical to ensuring that AI is developed and used in ways that benefit humanity as a whole.
- o **Example**: **Global AI initiatives**, such as the **OECD's AI principles** or the **UN's AI for Good**, aim to create guidelines for responsible AI development and deployment that can be adopted worldwide, promoting fairness and reducing the risk of harm across borders.

Innovating Responsibly: Striking the Right Balance Between Progress and Responsibility

As AI continues to push the boundaries of innovation, it is crucial that the development of new technologies is balanced with **responsibility**. Ethical AI design requires considering the broader societal implications of AI systems, ensuring that progress does not come at the expense of human rights, fairness, or the environment.

1. **The Ethics of AI Innovation**:
    o   Rapid technological progress often comes with unforeseen ethical dilemmas. Striking the right balance between innovation and responsibility requires developers, companies, and policymakers to think ahead about the potential consequences of their work. For example, in the race to create **autonomous AI systems**, ethical issues such as **privacy**, **accountability**, and **safety** need to be considered alongside technical challenges like performance and efficiency.
    o   **Example**: In developing **AI in healthcare**, while AI may improve diagnosis and treatment, the ethical implications of data privacy and consent, as well as ensuring equitable access to these technologies, must also be addressed.
2. **Inclusive and Responsible AI Design**:
    o   Responsible innovation involves designing AI systems that are inclusive,

equitable, and accessible. Developers need to prioritize **inclusive design** to ensure that AI technologies work for all people, regardless of race, gender, ability, or socioeconomic status. This also includes being transparent about the ways AI systems may influence people's lives and ensuring that those affected have a say in how these systems are used.

- o **Example**: For AI in education, responsible innovation means designing systems that are accessible to students from different backgrounds, including those with disabilities or those living in areas with limited technological access.

3. **Corporate Social Responsibility (CSR) and AI**:
    - o As AI becomes an integral part of industries such as finance, healthcare, and marketing, companies must adopt **corporate social responsibility** (CSR) practices to ensure that their AI systems are developed ethically. This includes **evaluating the social impact** of AI technologies, prioritizing **sustainability**, and avoiding harmful outcomes like **algorithmic discrimination**.
    - o **Example**: In the financial sector, companies must be careful to design AI systems that do not unfairly exclude underrepresented groups from financial services (e.g., loans or insurance) based on biased data.

4. **AI Ethics and Regulation**:
   - Government regulation will play a critical role in ensuring responsible innovation. Ethical AI design cannot rely solely on companies or developers—it requires a robust regulatory environment that defines **ethical standards** and holds AI developers accountable for the impact of their systems. Balancing regulation with innovation will be key to ensuring that AI benefits society while mitigating risks.
   - **Example**: The **European Union's AI Act** aims to regulate high-risk AI applications by setting clear rules for transparency, accountability, and fairness, ensuring that AI technologies are developed in a way that aligns with public values.

Building a Better Future with AI: The Role of Ethical AI in Shaping a Just Society

AI has the potential to create significant benefits for society, but these benefits can only be realized if AI is developed in a way that prioritizes **justice**, **equality**, and **human dignity**. The future of ethical AI design will be shaped by efforts to ensure that AI systems are used for the greater good, addressing global challenges and promoting a more just and sustainable society.

1. **AI for Social Good**:
   - One of the most exciting possibilities for AI in the future is its potential to address

some of the world's most pressing **social challenges**. AI can be used to improve **healthcare**, address **climate change**, promote **education**, and reduce **inequality**. Ensuring that AI is developed for the **public good** requires the collaboration of governments, companies, researchers, and civil society to create AI systems that benefit everyone.

o **Example**: AI applications are being used to track and predict the spread of diseases, such as **COVID-19**, helping governments and healthcare providers respond more effectively to public health crises. Similarly, AI is being used to **optimize energy consumption** and **reduce carbon footprints**, contributing to efforts to combat climate change.

2. **AI and Human Rights**:

o As AI continues to influence various aspects of society, it must be aligned with **human rights principles**. This means designing AI systems that promote **freedom**, **equality**, and **privacy**, and ensuring that AI does not violate or undermine fundamental rights. AI must serve as a tool for **empowerment** and **social justice**, not as a mechanism of control or exclusion.

o **Example**: **AI for social justice** initiatives, such as those aimed at improving access to legal services or reducing bias in the criminal justice system, demonstrate how AI can be used to promote human rights and fairness.

3. **Sustainability and Ethical AI**:

   o The development of AI must be aligned with **sustainable development goals** (SDGs), ensuring that AI systems are designed to support long-term environmental, economic, and social sustainability. Ethical AI will play a critical role in **environmental sustainability**, reducing waste, optimizing resources, and minimizing environmental harm.

   o **Example**: AI applications are being used in **smart grids** to optimize energy use and reduce waste, contributing to a more sustainable energy future. Additionally, AI-driven solutions are being applied to monitor and protect **biodiversity** and **natural resources**, ensuring that development does not come at the expense of the environment.

Real-World Example: Ethical AI in Environmental Sustainability and Global Challenges

AI has already demonstrated its potential to tackle **global challenges**, particularly in the areas of **environmental sustainability** and **climate change**. AI-driven solutions are helping to reduce environmental impacts, optimize resource use, and promote sustainability in industries like agriculture, energy, and waste management.

1. **AI in Climate Change Mitigation**:
   o AI is being used to model climate change scenarios, optimize **renewable energy production**, and reduce carbon emissions. AI-powered systems can predict weather patterns, optimize the distribution of energy from solar and wind farms, and help governments and organizations make data-driven decisions on climate action.
   o **Example**: Companies like **DeepMind** have applied AI to reduce the energy consumption of data centers, significantly cutting down on their carbon footprint. Similarly, AI is being used to optimize the performance of **solar panels** and **wind turbines**, ensuring that renewable energy sources are utilized efficiently.
2. **AI in Sustainable Agriculture**:
   o AI applications are also being used in **agriculture** to improve crop yields, reduce water consumption, and minimize the environmental impact of farming. AI systems can analyze soil health, optimize irrigation, and monitor pest populations, leading to more sustainable agricultural practices.
   o **Example**: AI-powered systems in **precision agriculture** help farmers use resources more efficiently, increasing food production while reducing waste and environmental degradation.
3. **AI for Disaster Response**:

- o AI is playing a critical role in **disaster response** by analyzing data from satellites, drones, and social media to help authorities respond to natural disasters more effectively. AI-driven systems can predict the impact of events like hurricanes, earthquakes, or wildfires, enabling faster and more accurate responses.
- o **Example**: AI tools are used to analyze satellite imagery to identify areas affected by **flooding**, **wildfires**, or **hurricanes**, allowing emergency responders to allocate resources efficiently and minimize harm to affected communities.

Summary

In this chapter, we explored the **future of ethical AI design**, focusing on emerging challenges and future directions in AI ethics. As AI technology continues to evolve, addressing complex ethical issues such as **bias**, **accountability**, and **global governance** will be critical to ensuring that AI serves humanity responsibly.

We discussed the importance of **innovating responsibly**, balancing progress with ethical considerations, and ensuring that AI contributes to a **just society**. AI has the potential to address pressing global challenges, from **climate change** to **healthcare**, but it must be developed in ways that prioritize **human rights, sustainability,** and **social justice**.

The chapter also provided a **real-world example** of how AI is being used in **environmental sustainability**, demonstrating how ethical AI can contribute to mitigating climate change, optimizing resource use, and addressing global challenges. As AI becomes an integral part of solving global issues, it is crucial that ethical considerations remain at the forefront, ensuring that AI technologies benefit all of humanity in a fair and responsible way.

www.ingramcontent.com/pod-product-compliance
Lightning Source LLC
LaVergne TN
LVHW022337060326
832902LV00022B/4085